W9-BLO-708

m/H
0223

BETRAYAL

BETRAYAL

THE HITLER-STALIN PACT OF 1939

Wolfgang Leonhard

Translated by Richard D. Bosley

St. Martin's Press | New York

BETRAYAL: THE HITLER-STALIN PACT OF 1939. Copyright © 1986 by Wolfgang Leonhard. Translation copyright © 1989 by St. Martin's Press, Inc. All rights reserved. Printed in the United States of America. No part of this book may be used or reproduced in any manner whatsoever without written permission except in the case of brief quotations embodied in critical articles or reviews. For information, address St. Martin's Press, 175 Fifth Avenue, New York, N.Y. 10010.

Library of Congress Cataloging-in-Publication Data

Leonhard, Wolfgang.
    Betrayal : the Hitler-Stalin pact of 1939.
       p. cm.
    ISBN 0-312-02868-7
    1. World War, 1939–1945—Diplomatic history.
  2. Germany—Foreign relations—Soviet Union. 3. Soviet Union—Foreign relations—Germany. I. Title.
D751.L4 1989 940.53'2—dc19 89-4074

First Edition
10 9 8 7 6 5 4 3 2 1

Contents

INTRODUCTION:
THE CURRENT DISCUSSION OF
THE HITLER-STALIN PACT
IN THE SOVIET UNION

The events described in this book transpired half a century ago: On August 23, 1989, the world will mark the 50th year since the Hitler-Stalin pact was signed. As we shall see, this agreement was not, primarily, a nonaggression pact between Nazi Germany and the Soviet Union, as the Soviets maintain. Of much greater importance were the agreements in the Secret Additional Protocol governing the allocation of sovereign states in Eastern Europe to the two authoritarian powers.

The four articles of the Secret Protocol provided for the partition of Poland between Nazi Germany and the Soviet Union. The rivers Narev, Vistula, and San were to delineate the spheres of interest of these two powers. Bessarabia, which was a part of Rumania, was alloted to the Soviet Union. The Secret Protocol also sealed the fate of the three Baltic Republics: Estonia and Latvia fell to the Soviet Union, and Lithuania to the German Reich. However, only five weeks later, on September 29, 1939, the Secret Protocol was amended to increase Germany's sphere of influence in Poland, in exchange for which the German Reich ceded Lithuania to the USSR.

The terms of the Secret Protocol were quickly implemented: On September 1, 1939, Germany attacked Poland, while on September 17, Soviet troops occupied the Soviet sphere of interest in Eastern Poland. Poland was effectively partitioned between the two powers: The German portion of Poland was administered by a Governor General, while in the territory occupied by the Soviet Union a "plebiscite" was organized in which the populace "voted" for a union with the Soviet Union.

In the autumn of 1939, the Soviet Union established military bases in the Baltic Republics of Estonia, Latvia, and Lithuania, which had been ceded to it by the Secret Protocol. The complete military occupation of these three independent nations took place in the middle of June 1940. As in Poland, controlled plebiscites were organized, in which the populace voted for union with the USSR. Estonia, Latvia, and Lithuania became union republics.

Finally, at the beginning of August 1940, Soviet troops occupied Bessarabia in the northeastern part of Rumania. Shortly thereafter, Bessarabia was annexed to the Soviet Union as the Moldavian Union Republic.

The Secret Additional Protocol remained, as is discussed at the end of Chapter 1, completely secret. The fourteen members of the German Embassy in Moscow were obliged to swear in writing neither to reveal the contents of the Secret Protocol—which were known by only three or four of them anyway—nor even to mention the existence of "a certain secret protocol." This declaration of secrecy was dated August 27, 1939, and was placed in an envelope sealed with wax. Microfilms of the Secret Protocol were made in the office of Foreign Minister von Ribbentrop. When the allies began to bomb Berlin, the originals and the microfilms of the agreements were frequently evacuated. Many of the files of the Ministry of Foreign Affairs were destroyed on purpose during the last months of the war, but the microfilms of the documents were preserved, including that of the Secret

Additional Protocol annexed to the nonaggression pact of August 23, 1939. At the end of the war, all of this material fell into the hands of the Western allies. American and British experts had never doubted for a moment that this archival material was genuine. It was first collected in Marburg and then brought to Berlin. During the Berlin blockade of 1948, the files were flown to the United States. That year, the Department of State published these materials in English and in German in a book entitled *Nazi-Soviet Relations 1939–1941*.[1]

Some of the archives of the German Ministry of Foreign Affairs were located by the end of the war in the Soviet sector of Germany and were confiscated by Soviet troops. They are reportedly now in the state archives of the German Democratic Republic in Potsdam. Some of the documents concerning the Hitler-Stalin pact must also be in Moscow, although to this day it is not known in which archive they are kept and whether or not the Ministry of Foreign Affairs or the Central State Archival Administration will release them.

During the Stalin era, neither the Secret Additional Protocol to the nonaggression pact nor the amendment to the Secret Protocol, signed by von Ribbentrop in Moscow on September 29, 1939, could be quoted or even mentioned. Nor did this change after Stalin's death on March 5, 1953. During the period of de-Stalinization under Khrushchev, from 1953 until 1964, Stalin was accused of many crimes, not only in Khrushchev's "secret speech," delivered on February 25, 1956, but also during the 22nd Party Congress in October 1961. Nevertheless, the Hitler-Stalin pact continued to be justified as a nonaggression pact. This interpretation remained unchanged during the Brezhnev era, which lasted almost twenty years, from October 1964 until the middle of the 1980s.

A gradual change only became apparent after Mikhail Gorbachev was appointed General Secretary of the CPSU on March

11, 1985. Little by little, historians, journalists, and writers began to discuss certain aspects of the Stalin era which had been taboo until then. The collectivization of agriculture, the Great Purge of 1936–1938, Stalin's grave errors during the Second World War, and the suppression of intellectuals were discussed more frequently and in greater detail than before.

General Secretary Gorbachev promoted this critical review of the Stalin era when he declared at a conference attended by representatives of the media on February 14, 1987, "that there should neither be forgotten names nor blank spots in our history and literature." As a result, Soviet historians, writers, and journalists also began to examine the Hitler-Stalin pact. On April 26, 1987, Gorbachev and General Jaruzelski, the Polish head of state, signed an accord which instructed the historians of both countries to clarify the "blank spots" in their history. With that, a discussion of the Hitler-Stalin pact and the subsequent partition of Poland could no longer be avoided.

In the summer of 1987, the question of the Hitler-Stalin pact was raised in the three Baltic Republics of the USSR—Lithuania, Latvia, and Estonia—which had been occupied and annexed in June of 1940 as a direct result of the Secret Protocol. August 23, 1987, the 48th anniversary of the signing of the pact in Moscow, was marked by demonstrations in the three Baltic capitals: Tallinn (Estonia), Riga (Latvia), and Vilnius (Lithuania). The Soviet press considered these demonstrations to be a negative phenomenon.

Only a few weeks later, on October 9, 1987, the Polish journal *Zycie Literacki* published the Secret Protocol for the first time in the Eastern bloc. The commentary explained that the Soviets had unfortunately not yet published this historic document. Many people hoped that Gorbachev would critically address the Hitler-Stalin pact in his speech on the occasion of the 70th anniversary of the Great October Revolution, delivered on November 2, 1987. However, this hope remained unfulfilled: Gorbachev continued to justify the pact, albeit in a somewhat milder form than usual, and failed to mention the Secret Protocol, apparently because of resistance from the top levels of the party.

The critical assessment of the Stalin era began to increase in the spring of 1988. The rehabilitation of Bukharin and other victims of the show trials of 1936–1938 produced more publications on Stalin's terror and, especially since the summer of 1988, a more critical assessment of Stalin's foreign policy. The Soviet historian Vasily Kulish, for example, explained in a widely read article in the *Komsomolskaya Pravda* on August 23, 1988, that at the beginning of the 1930s, Soviet leaders forwarded two opposing foreign policy doctrines. Stalin and his closest colleagues—Molotov, Voroshilov, Kaganovich, and Malenkov—believed that the Soviet Union was threatened by a "capitalist encirclement." German Fascism was considered only a variety of imperialism. This view was opposed by Bukharin (executed in March 1938), Foreign Minister Litvinov (demoted in May 1939), and by the General Staff under Marshal Tukhachevsky (shot in June 1937), who considered Fascism a fundamentally new phenomenon and who therefore advocated an alliance with the Western democracies against Hitler. The treaty of Munich, which effectively ceded Czechoslovakia to the Nazis, helped lead to the defeat of the second view.

The main element behind the further development of Soviet foreign policy was Stalin's false assessment of German Fascism. In the beginning, the Soviet Union had always accused Great Britain and France of not actively seeking an alliance with the USSR against Hitler. Later on, however, Kulish explained, the Great Purge had so weakened the USSR that an alliance with such a weak partner would have been an unbearable risk to

Great Britain and France. Stalin, on the other hand, was less interested in an alliance since he believed that Britain and France themselves were too weak to oppose Nazi Germany.

In its September 1988 issue, the journal *Druzhba Narodov* published a letter written by an expert on Soviet foreign policy, Ernst Henry, to Ilya Ehrenburg on May 30, 1965, which had been kept secret until then. In this letter, Henry considered the Hitler-Stalin pact within the context of all of Stalin's erroneous assessments of German Fascism. The first of these errors occurred in 1924, when Stalin branded the Social Democrats as "Fascism's moderate wing" and explained: "We don't need a coalition with Social Democracy, but a life and death struggle with it."[2]

The consequences of such a view were, in Henry's opinion, devastating:

> The old Social Democrats from the ranks of the workers were not just deeply offended, but downright furious. They could not forgive the Communists for this, and the Communists gnashed their teeth as they executed the order for a "life and death struggle," since an order is an order and Party discipline is Party discipline. To the delight of the Fascists, Social Democrats and Communists fought against one another everywhere. I remember it well, since I lived in Germany at the time and will never forget how the old comrades clenched their fists in silence when they saw that everything had changed and that the theory of "Social Fascism" was paving the way for Hitler.

Ernst Henry also described the catastrophic effect which the Hitler-Stalin pact had on the Communist parties of Europe:

> When Stalin concluded the pact with Hitler in 1939 and ordered the Communist parties throughout the world to stop

their anti-Fascist propaganda immediately and to begin supporting a peaceful agreement with Hitler the situation became very grave. . . . Stalin did not limit himself to splitting the Social Democrats from the Communists, but began to disarm and discredit the Communists in the West.

After Ernst Henry's letter was published in *Druzhba Narodov*, it was published in the German-language Soviet magazine *Sputnik*, with the result that on November 21, 1988, the censors in the German Democratic Republic forbade the distribution of this issue in East Germany.[3]

In August 1988, the Secret Protocol was published officially in the three Baltic Republics. On August 10 and 11, the newspaper of the Estonian CP, *Rava Hääl*, published the text of the Secret Protocol and a commentary by the Estonian historian Heino Arumää. One week later, the text of the Secret Protocol and a slightly shortened version of Arumää's article were published in Russian in Estonia's Russian-language newspaper *Sovetskaya Estoniya*, together with the famous photograph of Stalin, Molotov, and von Ribbentrop toasting. Shortly thereafter, a film of the signing of the nonaggression pact on August 23, 1939, was shown for the first time on Soviet television—but again only in Estonia.

The Secret Protocol was published at the same time, albeit with a smaller circulation, in the Lithuanian newspaper *Literatura Ir Minas* on August 20, 1988, and in Russian in the Russian-language Lithuanian journal *Vestnik Litovskogo dvizheniya za perestrojku* (no. 4, 1988). And so, paradoxically, the Secret Protocol was published in Estonian, Lithuanian, and in Russian in publications distributed in those two republics, but not in the rest of the Soviet Union.

The subsequent course of events was particularly influenced by the demonstrations in the Baltic Republics on the occasion of the 49th anniversary of the signing of the pact. In Estonia, the demonstration was organized by the Estonian Popular Front, which has since been legalized, in the capital, Tallinn. The rally took place in a convention hall amid a sea of blue, black, and white banners, the national flag of Estonia, which has also been legalized since then. The Estonian Popular Front invited not only Estonian speakers but also the revisionist Soviet historian Yuri Afanassyev, who admitted not only the existence of the Secret Protocol but that it had led to the occupation of Estonia by the Soviet Union. Afanassyev stated that no one could seriously claim that the Baltic Republics had voluntarily agreed to be united with the Soviet Union in the summer of 1940. "We are speaking of historical injustice," he explained, "about which one cannot remain silent. In no other country has history been falsified to such a degree as in the Soviet Union. Every school child in the West knows about these protocols, but we still deny them, or rather, we continue to deny their existence."

On August 23, 1988, about 60,000 people took part in an authorized demonstration in Riga, the capital of Latvia. Most of the participants were Latvians, but there were also Estonians, Russians, and Armenians. Eyewitnesses reported that they had not only seen the dark red, white, and red banner of Latvia, which had been outlawed until then, but also Polish, Lithuanian, and Finnish flags. Among the many speakers, Mavriks Wulfsons, a political commentator who for some time had demanded an open discussion of the Hitler-Stalin pact, was greeted with particular enthusiasm. Estonian and Armenian representatives also spoke. Some of the Latvian speakers spoke Russian so that the non-Latvians could understand. The speech by the Russian Sergei Igoryonuk was also well received: Igoryonuk explained that all citizens should recognize that Latvia belongs to the Latvians, who have the right to determine the future of their country. Moreover, he also opposed all forms of Great Russian chauvinism. The head of the Helsinki-86 group in Latvia, Dr. Juris Vidins, criticized the Soviet leaders for their suppression of human rights in the republic.

The Latvian Andris Zukovskis read a letter written by several American senators on August 17, 1988, to General Secretary Gorbachev, urging him to publish and officially condemn the Secret Protocol. This letter was enthusiastically received by the listeners. The demonstration ended with the singing of the Latvian national anthem, "God Save Latvia," which had been forbidden until then.

The demonstration in Vingis Park in Vilnius, the capital of Lithuania, was particularly impressive. Some 100,000 people attended. The Hitler-Stalin pact was the focus of most of the speeches, the transcript of which was published in Lithuanian and in Russian; the latter version was published in the magazine of the popular movement *Vozrozhdenie/Rebirth*. During the course of this demonstration, the Lithuanian musicologist Vytautas Landsbergis explained that "on this day two people signed a document. Their names were Molotov and von Ribbentrop. But behind these two dangerous criminals stood two others: Hitler and Stalin, both of whom stood for inhuman policies and actions and for two systems—Nazism and Stalinism—which did not limit themselves to domestic crimes but which expanded in a wave of blood into other territories." The victories of one dictator had whetted the appetite of the other. It was the task of those present to recall the events of the past. Moreover, Landsbergis considered it laudable that historians had more freedom, since only when the people had overcome the heritage of Stalinism could they proceed to solve other problems of life.

The Lithuanian poet Justinias Marcinkevicius recalled the photograph that was published in the Soviet press forty-nine years ago—Stalin raising his glass of champagne and congratulating Molotov and von Ribbentrop after they had signed the nonaggression pact. This treaty had had frightful consequences for the Communist and Social Democratic parties of Europe. Even the Soviet populace had accepted the treaty cautiously and with resignation. They were right to do so, for only one week after the champagne and the congratulatory addresses of Stalin, Molotov, and von Ribbentrop, the Second World War began. Marcinkevicius recalled that the Soviet Union had shipped huge quantities of oil and other strategic materials to Nazi Germany. The Comintern had applauded the pact even though it destroyed the anti-Fascist front comprising all the progressive forces in the West. European Communists in Moscow were arrested and some perished. The leader of the German Communists, Ernst Thälmann, who could have been freed from a death camp, was abandoned. Eighteen months later, Hitler invaded the Soviet Union. The signing of the pact on August 23, 1939, was a strategic error of Soviet foreign policy and marked, for all practical purposes, the beginning of the Second World War. Consequently, the pact should be condemned unconditionally. At the end of his speech, Marcinkevicius demanded that the Hitler-Stalin pact, including the Secret Additional Protocol, be published and officially condemned.

Antanas Buracas, a member of the Lithuanian Academy of Sciences, explained that half a century had passed since the signing of the Hitler-Stalin pact. The era of colonialist imperialism was over, and international relations were based on principles of genuine equality. Therefore, it was time to cement the sovereignty of Lithuania in law and to guarantee it the right to develop as it sees fit.

Even the Secretary of the Central Committee of the CP Lithuania, Lionginas Sepetys, spoke at the demonstration. He recalled that the listeners had just honored the victims of Stalinism with a moment of silence. However, the promise to erect a monument to the victims of Stalinism remained unfulfilled. As a party secretary, he declared openly that he would take all necessary measures to give restitution to and rehabilitate the victims of the deportations: "Here and now in the Vingis Park we condemn the theory and the practice of Stalinism and Hitlerism."

The Lithuanian historian Gedeminas Rudis explained that representatives of the two most reactionary regimes of the twentieth century had sat at the negotiating table on August 23, 1939: the Stalinist and the Nazi. Both had violated the fundamental norms of international law and allocated sovereign states to their spheres of influence. Shortly thereafter, Poland ceased to exist. Under the pretense that a "revolutionary situation" had existed in Lithuania, Latvia, and Estonia, in June of 1940, all three Baltic Republics were occupied. Rudis supported the proposal forwarded by Soviet members of the Academy of Sciences that the Secret Protocol be published, and he rejected the assertions of certain historians and archivists who maintain that the originals of the Secret Protocol and the amendment thereto could not be found. The Secret Protocol has not only been known in the West for decades but even published in Estonia and Latvia. However he declared that it was not enough to simply publish the Secret Protocol: "What we need is a serious, historical analysis." This is particularly true of the period around June 14, 1940, when the Baltic Republics were occupied. The claims that Lithuanians supposedly attacked Red Army soldiers were clearly false, for neither Lithuania, Latvia, nor Estonia had ever threatened the Soviet Union.

After this, a tape recording made by Lithuania's former Minister of Foreign Affairs, the ninety-two-year-old Juoazas Urbsys, was played to the 100,000 listeners. Urbsys recalled his talks with Molotov and Stalin at the time of the Hitler-Stalin pact. Then the historian Luido Struska recalled the results of the occupation of Lithuania: the suppression, the mass deportations, the murders, the destruction of culture and the economy, and the national humiliation. All of the citizens of Lithuania—Lithuanians, Jews, Poles, and Russians—who were deported and tortured in prisons as well as those who died after the war were all victims of the Hitler-Stalin pact.

The demonstrations on August 23, 1988, in Riga, Tallinn, and Vilnius broached the topic of the Hitler-Stalin pact and its consequences. Soviet citizens far beyond the borders of the three Baltic Republics began to discuss the pact and demand that the Secret Protocol be published. The speaker of the Soviet Foreign Ministry, Gerassimov, declared that no copies of the Secret Protocol could be found in Soviet archives, and even the originals apparently no longer existed. The Soviet press agency TASS once again defended the nonaggression pact, calling it a measure necessitated by the historical situation. Several days later, however, the first small steps were taken toward historical truth: The nonaggression pact was still defended, but the Friendship and Border Treaty signed on September 29, 1939, was critically assessed for the first time. The commentary said: "In September of the same year (1939) Stalin concluded a Treaty of Friendship with Germany. A friendship treaty with Fascism? How is one to interpret that? After Hitler's witch hunt of German Communists, his interference in Spain? Is one to consider the conclusion of such a treaty the zenith of a statesman's wisdom?"[4]

The discussions, therefore, continue, and the end is not yet in sight. Should the policy of glasnost and reforms continue, then one may expect that at last on August 23, 1989, fifty years after the Hitler-Stalin pact was signed, the Secret Protocol will finally be published and the pact itself revealed for what it really was: The agreement of two dictatorships to define their spheres of influence, which led to the occupation of independent nations and which was of decisive importance for the outbreak of the

Second World War. In short, the Soviet populace would finally be informed of this tragic event, 50 years after the fact.

One can only hope that, if the protocols are published, the commentary will not be limited to the foreign policy aspects but will describe the tragedies which this treaty brought to individuals, in particular to anti-Fascists. One can only hope that the party's leaders will recall the shock and bewilderment of anti-Fascists around the world, whose experiences and reactions are the subject of this book.

1

THE HANDSHAKE IN MOSCOW: SECRECY AND SURPRISE AT THE HIGHEST LEVEL

Von Ribbentrop Meets with Stalin and Molotov

The secrecy surrounding Foreign Minister von Ribbentrop's journey to Moscow on August 23, 1939, was so complete that there were only a few eyewitnesses, and of these only one has left a firsthand account of the event. The *Pravda* reported that the German delegation comprised von Ribbentrop, Gaus, Baron von Dörnberg, Paul Schmidt, Prof. Dr. G. Hoffmann, K. Schnurre, "and others." They were greeted at the Moscow airport by the Soviet Deputy Minister of Foreign Affairs, V. P. Potemkin; the Deputy Minister of Trade, M. S. Stepanov; the Deputy Minister of the Interior, V. N. Merkulov; the Chairman of the Moscow City Council (Soviet); "and others." According to the *Pravda*, members of the German Embassy, "led by Ambassador von der Schulenburg," were present, as well as the Italian ambassador and his military attaché.

None of the Soviet officials left memoirs that describe von Ribbentrop's visit and negotiations. Fortunately, a German witness to these decisive events left an objective and reliable account of the meeting—Hans von Herwarth, then attached to the German Embassy in Moscow, was a critic and later opponent of the Nazi regime.

Von Herwarth was born in Berlin in 1904 but spent his childhood in the German province of Posnania. In 1918, he returned with his parents to Berlin, attended school there, and then worked as a laborer in locomotive factories. Years later, he described how important it was to learn what it means to work an eight-hour day. He came to know the workers in their own milieu, witnessed the activity of the trade unions, and observed the often stormy discussions between the mainstream Social Democrats, the leftist "Independent Social Democrats," and the Communists. Thereafter, he studied law in Breslau (today Wroclaw) and Munich and, after passing the bar exam, obtained a position in the Ministry of Foreign Affairs in 1927.

At the end of May 1931, von Herwarth was posted to the German Embassy in Moscow. He attentively observed the First Five Year Plan and the collectivization of Soviet agriculture. He not only became acquainted with the life of the Soviet people but also met higher Soviet officials, (almost all of whom later perished during the Great Purge of 1936–1938). He met frequently with disillusioned foreign Communists, among them Max Hölz.

Von Herwarth quickly established an amicable relationship with Graf von der Shulenburg, who was appointed Ambassador to Moscow in October 1934. He was, therefore, not only a witness to, but in part a participant in, the improvement of German-Soviet relations, which began in the spring of 1939 and which led to von Ribbentrop's visit almost five years later.

On August 23, 1939, Hans von Herwarth waited at the Moscow airport with another member of the German Embassy, Gebhardt von Walther. He recalled, above all, the way the Gestapo men greeted their counterparts from the Soviet secret police, then known as the NKVD (People's Commission for Internal Affairs).

> Upon his arrival in Moscow, von Ribbentrop was welcomed by a group of Soviet officials and by Graf Schulenburg. I was standing next to Gebhardt von Walther and we both eagerly watched this first German-Soviet meeting from which the public was excluded. Walther seized my arm and pointed to a group of Gestapo agents who warmly greeted their counterparts from the NKVD. "Look at how they laugh. They're pleased that they can finally cooperate. That could be frightful. Just imagine if they exchanged files."[1]

The German-Soviet negotiations began that day at 3:00 P.M. The Soviet delegation included Stalin and Molotov; the German delegation, von Ribbentrop, von der Schulenburg, and Hilger. Von Ribbentrop transmitted a message from Hitler that stated "from now on all of the problems of Eastern Europe should be exclusively the concern of Germany and Russia." Stalin immediately broached the topic that was most important to him: The USSR demanded the Latvian ports of Liepaja (Libau) and Ventspils (Windau). Von Ribbentrop telephoned Hitler to obtain his consent and permission to sign the secret agreement that would delimit each country's sphere of influence. Hitler ordered that an atlas be brought to him in haste, looked at the map, and at about 8:00 P.M. answered: "yes, agreed."

The meeting was resumed in the evening and lasted until after midnight. Hans von Herwarth spent these hours in the residence of the German ambassador to ensure the immediate transmission of messages between Moscow and Berlin. He recalled the following: "A direct telephone line was established between Moscow and Berlin. Several times I had to obtain Hitler's consent to changes in the text of the agreement, especially for small changes in the proposed border. I was surprised at how quickly Hitler consented so that the agreement would be concluded as quickly as possible." However, von Herwarth learned even more during this peculiar night—for example, that Stalin had personally conducted the negotiations for the Soviet side. Stalin made no secret to von Ribbentrop of the fact that he had long favored a rapprochement between the USSR and Germany.

The nonaggression pact and the Secret Protocol, dated August 23, 1939, were signed at 2:00 A.M. on August 24. Shortly thereafter, photographers were admitted to record the historic moment: Their cameras showed that the participants were satisfied and smiling. Champagne corks popped; Stalin toasted Hitler: "I know how much the German people love their Führer, and that is why I have the pleasure of drinking to his health!"[2] Stalin raised his glass to Hitler and called him a *molodets*, or "fine fellow."

Von Herwarth recalled that the German photographer Helmut Laux was among those present: Laux "later described to me how he photographed von Ribbentrop and Stalin. Each had a glass of champagne in his hand and was drinking to the success of the agreement. Stalin commented that it would not be wise to release this photograph, since it could make a false impression on the German and Soviet peoples. Laux started to open his camera to give Stalin the film but Stalin waved him away, saying that the word of a German was enough for him."[3]

On August 24, von Ribbentrop departed from Moscow at 1:25 P.M., seen off by the same Soviet officials who had greeted him the previous day. He returned to Berlin and informed Hitler the same afternoon. Hitler was extremely pleased and heaped praise on his foreign minister. Now nothing could stop the outbreak of war; Germany was preparing frenetically for the invasion of Poland.[4]

The *Pravda* Publishes the Nonaggression Pact

The *Pravda* reported the signing of the nonaggression pact on August 24. It was one of the most astonishing issues of the *Pravda* in the history of the Soviet Union.

Big front-page pictures in the *Pravda* showed Molotov, Stalin, von Ribbentrop, and Gaus, the Deputy Secretary of State at the German Foreign Office and its legal adviser, and an interpreter. . . . Below the picture of the Kremlin meeting there was this announcement:

At 3:30 P.M. on August 23 a first conversation took place between . . . V. M. Molotov and the Foreign Minister of Germany Herr von Ribbentrop. The conversation took place in the presence of Comrade Stalin and the German Ambassador Count von der Schulenburg. It lasted about three hours. After a rest the conversation was resumed at 10 P.M. and ended with the signing of the Treaty of Non-Aggression, the text of which follows:

The Government of the German Reich and
The Government of the Union of Soviet Socialist Republics
Desirous of strengthening the cause of peace between Germany and the U.S.S.R., and proceeding from the fundamental provisions of the Neutrality Agreement concluded in April, 1926 between Germany and the U.S.S.R., have reached the following Agreement:
Article I. Both High Contracting Parties obligate themselves to desist from any act of violence, any aggressive

action, and any attack on each other, either individually or jointly with other Powers.

Article II. Should one of the High Contracting Parties become the object of belligerent action by a third Power, the other High Contracting Party shall in no manner lend its support to this third Power.

Article III. The Governments of the two High Contracting Parties shall in the future maintain continual contact with one another for the purpose of consultation in order to exchange information on problems affecting their common interests.

Article IV. Neither of the two High Contracting Parties shall participate in any grouping of Powers whatsoever that is directly or indirectly aimed at the other party.

Article V. Should disputes or conflicts arise between the High Contracting Parties over problems of one kind or another, both parties shall settle these disputes or conflicts exclusively through friendly exchange of opinion or, if necessary, through the establishment of arbitration commissions.

Article VI. The present Treaty is concluded for a period of ten years, with the proviso that, in so far as one of the High Contracting Parties does not denounce it one year prior to the expiration of this period, the validity of this Treaty shall automatically be extended for another five years.

Article VII. The present treaty shall be ratified within the shortest possible time. The ratifications shall be exchanged in Berlin. The Agreement shall enter into force as soon as it is signed.

The editorial in the *Pravda* placed special emphasis on Article IV, which stipulated that neither party would participate in a grouping of powers aimed directly or indirectly at the other party. The editorial also highly commended Article V providing for the amicable settlement of disputes and the establishment of arbitration commissions.

On the following day, August 24, the *Pravda* briefly re- ported von Ribbentrop's departure at 1:25 P.M. The same people who had met him at the airport saw him off.[5]

Khruschev: The Members of the Politburo Were Hunting

One of the decisive questions connected with the Hitler-Stalin pact is this: Which of the Soviet leaders knew of and was involved in signing the agreement? The answer was provided by Nikita Khrushchev, who was then a member of the Politburo. Khrushchev was born in 1894 to a peasant family and joined the Bolshevik party in 1918. His first position was as Party Secretary of the Petrovo-Marinsk district in the Ukraine. In 1927, he advanced within the Ukrainian party organization and in 1929 was called to Moscow, where he was appointed Party Secretary of the Academy of Industry. In 1932, he became Second Secretary and in 1935, First Secretary of the Moscow party organization. He was appointed to the Central Committee in 1934 and to the Politburo of the CPSU in 1939. Khrushchev described the conclusion of the Hitler-Stalin pact in his memoirs, which were published thirty years later.

I was at Stalin's dacha on a Saturday, and he told me that Ribbentrop was flying in the next day. Stalin smiled and watched me closely to see what sort of an impression this news would make. At first I was dumbfounded. I stared back at him, thinking he was joking. Then I said, "Why should Ribbentrop want to see us? Is he defecting to our side, or what?"

"No," said Stalin, "Hitler has sent us a message saying, 'I ask you, Herr Stalin, to receive my minister Ribbentrop, who brings with him some concrete proposals.' We've agreed to meet with him tomorrow." I told Stalin that I'd already planned to go hunting with Bulganin and Malenkov at Voroshilov's preserve the next day. "Go right ahead. There'll be nothing for you to do around here tomorrow. Molotov and I will meet with Ribbentrop and hear what he has to say. When you come back from your hunt, I'll let you know what Hitler has in mind and what the outcome of our conversation with Ribbentrop is."

Later, Khrushchev went with Bulganin and Malenkov to the Zavidova game preserve. Voroshilov was already there when they arrived, which meant that he did not take part in the meeting with von Ribbentrop, even though as People's Commissar (Minister) for Defense he had been the head of several Soviet delegations in meetings with the Western powers. Now, however, he was excluded.

It is hard to believe, but true: the members of the Soviet Politburo were hunting. Khrushchev recalled that it had been a warm day and that the hunt had been a great success. He was especially pleased because he had bagged one duck more than Voroshilov—a seemingly significant feat, because the Soviet press had always featured Voroshilov as the best marksman in the Soviet Union. After the hunt, the members of the Politburo drove to Stalin's country house. Khruschev took his ducks in order to share them with the other members of the Politburo. He told Stalin about the hunt and boasted a bit about his success. Stalin was in good humor; Khrushchev recalled that

while the trophies of our hunt were being prepared for the table, Stalin told us that Ribbentrop had brought with him a draft of a friendship and nonaggression treaty which we had signed. Stalin seemed very pleased with himself. He said that when the English and French who were still in Moscow found out about the treaty the next day, they would immediately leave for home.

Stalin said, according to Khrushchev, that this agreement would delay the outbreak of war between Germany and the USSR for a while, with the result that the Soviet Union could remain neutral and strengthen its defense. After that, one would have to wait and see. In his memoirs, Khrushchev said he believed that the pact was, all in all, advantageous for the Soviet Union, because it had bought a breathing spell. He was, however, critical of the form of the treaty.

> We couldn't even discuss the treaty at Party meetings. For us to have explained our reasons for signing the treaty in straightforward newspaper language would have been offensive, and besides, nobody would have believed us. It was very hard for us—as Communists, as anti-Fascists, as people unalterably opposed to the philosophical and political position of the Fascists—to accept the idea of joining forces with Germany.[6]

Klement Gottwald Knew in Advance

Khrushchev's memoirs make it clear that, with the exception of Stalin and Molotov, even the members of the Soviet Politburo were not informed of the preparations for the nonaggression pact. But did anyone else in Moscow know about the agreement before it was made public? The answer is yes. The memoirs of Ernst Fischer reveal that several highly placed officials in the Communist International (Comintern) had at least received hints about the preparation of the pact. Among those who knew was Klement Gottwald.

Ernst Fischer (1899–1972) joined the Austrian Socialist Party in 1920, was editor of the socialist newspaper *Arbeiterzeitung* from 1927 until 1934, and in February 1934 took part in the uprising of the *Schutzbündler* in Vienna. He joined the Communist Party of Austria, emigrated to Prague and then to the Soviet Union, where he was active in the Comintern. He lived in the Hotel Lux, which was on Gorky Street in Moscow, and wrote articles and commentaries for radio under the pseudonym Peter Wieden. Forty years old at the time of the Hitler-Stalin pact, he recalled the following:

> On August 21 the *Pravda* published an editorial on the signing of trade and credit agreements with Germany. The article said that the agreements could bring about "a turning point in the economic relationships between both sides" and be "an important step in improving not only the economic but also the political relations between the USSR and Germany." I wanted to speak with Manuilski (the most important representative of the CPSU in the Comintern). In the corridor of the Comintern Gottwald waved me into his office. "Sit down," he said, and smiled a cunning, informed and vague smile.

Klement Gottwald, who was then forty-three, had been a member of the Central Committee of the Czechoslovak Communist party since October 1925. From 1926 until 1929, he directed the department of agitation and propaganda, and was then appointed to the Politburo. In February 1929, Gottwald became General Secretary of the Czechoslavak Communist party and a member of the Czech parliament. In July of that year, he joined the Presidium of the Executive Committee of the Communist International (ECCI), and, at the Seventh World Congress of the Communist International, held in the summer of 1935, he became a member of the ECCI Presidium and of the ECCI Secretariat. He moved, therefore, in the highest circles of the Comintern. He was again in Czechoslovakia from February 1936 until November 1938, but returned to Moscow as a result of the agreement signed by Chamberlain and Daladier in Munich. At the time of the Hitler-Stalin pact, Gottwald was the Comintern Secretary for Central Europe—that is, the territory directly affected by the agreement.

Fischer described his meeting with Gottwald on August 21, two days before the signing of the Hitler-Stalin pact.

> The leader of the Czech Communists, a cabinet-maker's apprentice from Vienna, was a man with a good knowledge of people, political instinct, and broad tactical experience. He liked to talk with me. Confidential discussions with me would by no means be detrimental, and could possibly be of value if I presented unexpected arguments which might be useful in future discussions with others. "What would you say," Gottwald squinted and made a wry face, "but don't tell anyone about it, I want to hear your opinion in confidence—do you understand, just between the two of us—what would you say if a bandit whom someone had paid to murder you suddenly offered to make an agreement?"

Gottwald continued in general terms and then came to the point. What would he, Ernst Fischer, say

> if Nazi Germany proposed a pact with the Soviet Union? . . . He watched my face closely and laughed strangely, half forced and half ill-at-ease, like a card player who puts his cards on the table without being certain that he has won. "Are you still there?" Gottwald continued. "Don't you believe me? Do you think that it's impossible . . . indecent . . . perfidious or what? And Munich . . . have you forgotten Munich? The four men in the conference room—Hitler, Mussolini, Chamberlain and Daladier."

Gottwald had talked himself into a rage: "Not even a year

has passed—do you understand—since Munich, since Czechoslovakia was torn to pieces. Herr von Ribbentrop was in Paris in December of 1938 and Monsieur Bonnet assured him that France had no interest in Eastern Europe and that Germany was free to do as she saw fit. The new project—the greater Ukraine. If you please, Herr Hitler, seize it. . . . But the robber . . . when the risk is too great, when he secretly informs the one he's supposed to murder: twenty years ago an arm and a leg was torn from you, a major part of the Ukraine and Byelorussia, in 1920 . . . the Poles, you know . . . if you take back what is yours and I don't assault you. . . ."

Ernst Fischer replied: "A partition of Poland?"

Gottwald answered: "Are you shocked? Yes? Speechless? It's not nice, to be sure, but in politics everyone has to look out for himself. . . . So, what do you think of a treaty with Germany?"

"Horrible," answered Fischer.

"It's a matter of life and death for the Soviet Union, do you understand?" replied Gottwald. "Can one afford to be so sensitive? Think about it, but don't tell anyone!"

Fischer followed this instruction: "I thought about it," he recorded in his memoirs.[7]

What Jesus Hernandez Learned from Dimitrij Manuilski

Ernst Fischer and Klement Gottwald were apparently the only ones who discussed the possibility of a treaty before it was concluded. All the other memoirs of Comintern officials deal with the period after the pact was announced. Of particular interest is the discussion the Spanish Communist party official Jesus Hernandez had with Dimitrij Manuilski in Kuntsevo immediately after the agreement was publicized.

Jesus Hernandez, who was thirty-two when the pact was signed, grew up in a poor family with five children in Bilbao. He joined the Spanish Communist party in 1922, when he was fifteen years old. He spent more than five years in prison. In 1931, after the proclamation of the Spanish Republic, he was invited to the Soviet Union and attended the Lenin School in Moscow, the main training center of the Comintern. He returned to Spain and worked in the Spanish CP's agitation and propaganda department and for the party newspaper, *Mundo Obrero*. In the elections of February 1936, from which the Popular Front emerged victorious, he was elected representative from Cordoba. During the Civil War from 1936 to 1939, Hernandez was Minister of Public Education in the Popular Front government— "Stalin's first minister abroad" he later wrote in his memoirs. At the same time, he was the political commissar for the armies of the central front. On the day before Franco entered Madrid, Hernandez fled together with other Communist party leaders to Algeria, from there to Le Havre, and then to the USSR, where he disembarked only a few months before the signing of the Hitler-Stalin pact.

His interlocutor was Dimitrij Manuilski (1883–1959). Manuilski became a Bolshevik in 1903, joined the Bolshevik underground under the pseudonym *Foma* ("Thomas"), and was arrested and banished several times until he finally fled to Paris. After the Bolshevik Revolution in November 1917, Manuilski was appointed a political commissar, and from 1919 on was primarily active in the international division of the Comintern. Under the pseudonym Ivanov he attended the congress of the German communists held in Frankfurt/Main in 1924. In the same year, he was appointed to the ECCI and to its Presidium. From 1928 on, he was the most important Soviet representative in the Comintern. Jesus Hernandez heard the news of the Hitler-Stalin pact in a country house (*dacha*) in Kuntsevo near Moscow, which was at the disposal of the top Comintern officials. He recorded his reaction to the news in his memoirs.

> For us Spanish von Ribbentrop dropped into Moscow like a bomb. The publication of photographs of Bolsheviks smiling at Nazis and the announcement that Germany and the USSR had signed a pact stupefied us. We had to rub our eyes to assure ourselves that we were in fact reading the *Pravda*.

Hernandez was particularly dismayed by two facts: first, that the agreement only mentioned the desire to preserve peace between Germany and the Soviet Union without mentioning peace in the rest of the world, and second, that the governments of the two countries would maintain close contacts and inform each other about all matters of mutual interest.

> On the same evening after hearing this shocking news I met Manuilski who lived in the same villa as I. I had known him long enough to risk questioning him about such things.
> "I am trying to understand this astounding shift!"
> "We had to gain time Hernandez."
> "But the pact frees Hitler's hands. That could have terrible consequences for the USSR."
> "Humpf! Our immediate goal is to eliminate Poland which has been a stepping stone for possible aggressors for much too long."
> "Eliminate Poland?"
> "That will be the first result of the pact. Poland will cease to exist as a country. We will have a common border with Germany." Manuilski smiled at my nonplussed expression.
> "But France and Germany have a treaty with Poland. That will mean war!"

"Only suicidal maniacs would dare to unleash a war against Germany and the USSR to defend Poland! Chamberlain and the others like him are too frightened to embark on such an enterprise. They'll kick and scream as they did at Munich, but I don't think that they'll vote for war."

"And if they do?"

"Everything has been taken care of. We can't lose!"

Since I didn't seem to be convinced he continued: "If the capitalists want to slit each other's throats, so much the better. When the time is right, when they begin to weary, we will undoubtedly be solicited by both sides and can choose the one which suits us best. Don't worry, our army won't pull the chestnuts out of the fire for any capitalist country."[8]

Castro Delgado: Excitement in the Comintern

Enrique Castro Delgado, the representative of the Spanish Communist party in the Comintern, described that memorable morning after the signing of the pact. He was thirty-two at the time, and had joined the Spanish Communist party in 1925, when he was eighteen. A few years later, he worked in the party's regional committee in Madrid and for the party newspaper *Mundo Obrero*. He was one of the organizers of the Communist Fifth Regiment during the Spanish Civil War and in 1937 was appointed to the Central Committee of the CP Spain, where he was primarily responsible for agrarian reform. However, he was also the commissar of the troops on the central front and directed the training of other political commissars.

After the defeat of the Spanish Republic in the spring of 1939, Delgado went to France and then to the USSR. At the time of the Hitler-Stalin pact, he was working in the Comintern under the pseudonym Luis Garcia and lived with his wife Esperanza in the Hotel Lux.

Since he didn't own an alarm clock, Delgado was accustomed to leaving the radio switched on at night so that he would be awakened by the first broadcast at 6:00 A.M. And so it was on the morning of August 24, 1939, only four hours after the pact was signed. "We were awakened by a march and then listened to the program of morning exercises—listened as one listens to the rain: the routine makes one indifferent."

Delgado listened for news about Spain, but nothing was mentioned. Instead, a deep, monotonous voice began to read something, to which he and his wife paid no attention. At the end they heard the names of Molotov and von Ribbentrop. They heard hurried steps in the next room, and they alone breakfasted in peace at 8:00.

I took my briefcase and went quickly down to the bus which left at 8:10. The scene I saw at the bus stop was different from that on most days: Today people didn't pile on board to get a seat. The stood in groups on the sidewalk and talked animatedly. Some were almost shouting.

I looked at one and then another. No one noticed me. I said "good morning" and no one answered. Everyone continued to talk, gesticulating and waving his arms. I was the only one who wasn't talking and gesticulating.

Of those waiting for the bus that brought the officials from the Hotel Lux to the Comintern, Castro Delgado was very likely the only one who knew nothing of the Hitler-Stalin pact. However, he was to learn of it very quickly, from Octavio Brandao, the representative of the Brazilian Communist party at the Comintern. Brandao was one of the cofounders of the CP Brazil in 1921; a poet and journalist by profession, he worked primarily in the party's agitation and propaganda department and in 1926 became a correspondent for Inprecor—short for *International Press Correspondence*, published by the Comintern. From 1932, Brandao lived in Moscow as the representative of the Brazilian Communist party.

This morning Brandao arrived as usual: running, tired, and one of the last to arrive. But Delgado noticed something unusual about him. "What a glint in his eyes, what a smile on his face!" Brandao went from one group to another; upon boarding the bus he saw Delgado, came up to him, and embraced him. Brandao pulled him into the middle of the bus: he shouted, smiled maliciously, and laughed. Brandao wanted to tell him something but had difficulty, since 50 Comintern officials were talking loudly in different languages. Finally Brandao drew near to him and said:

> Marvellous, comrade Luis, simply marvellous. . . . The Soviet Union has concluded a non-aggression pact and commercial agreement with Germany. Molotov and Ribbentrop signed for their governments. Marvellous, marvellous! The two camps, despite their contradictions . . . the Soviet Union developing in complete peace . . . marvellous, fantastic! They should destroy one another . . . that way our job will be easier. Fantastic, marvellous!

Finally the bus arrived at Rostokino, the Comintern building. This time the passengers were so excited that they paid no attention to the bridge or to the statue from the agricultural exhibition, or to the last curve before the entrance to the Comintern grounds. The passengers separated and disappeared faster than usual.[9]

Castro Delgado went to his office and broke the seals of a folder containing documents for him to read. He looked through other folders containing summaries of the foreign press and the correspondence of the Spanish collective.

At 11:00 A.M. they brought the official newsletter in Spanish and the *Pravda*. On page one of the *Pravda* there was
an enormous photograph of Stalin who seemed to be saying
to all the Communists of the world: "I did it, do you hear,
I!" I read the pact—once, twice, three times. I look at the
Pravda once, twice, three times. I think, and while I'm
thinking I seem to hear a soft but firm voice which repeats
untiringly:

"Stalin is right. Stalin never errs." I am convinced that in
299 offices 299 people are reading the newsletter and looking
at the *Pravda* and hearing a soft but firm voice repeat inces-
santly "Stalin is right. Stalin never errs."

Enrique Castro Delgado was dismayed and tried to find an
explanation. However, unlike other party officials, his primary
concern was not the foreign policy of the Soviet Union or Stalin's
decision, but Spain.

I am a Spaniard. Germany helped Franco gain power and
overthrow our republic. An airplane, a Messerschmitt, extin-
guished the life of my brother Manolo in a little village in
Catalonia with its machine guns. Hitler wants to dominate
Europe. . . . I am shocked by my thoughts . . . but I remember Spain. . . . If I could only forget it, if I could only
forget my brother, how he lay in the little room in a small
hospital, pale, serious . . . then I too would shout like these
fifty voices hammering at me. . . . But from Almeria to Guer-
nica, from Badajoz to Barcelona I hear the word "but" . . .
The dead . . . the dead . . . the dead. I look at the newsletter.
I look at the *Pravda*.

During the day, Delgado received, as did all other Comintern officials, the important news that at 6:00 P.M. a member
of the Central Committee of the Communist Party of the Soviet

Union would speak to the Comintern on the international situation.[10]

Ernst Fischer With Senior Members of the German Communist Party

Ernst Fischer also recalled the photograph of Stalin, Molotov,
and von Ribbentrop smiling on the front page of the *Pravda* on
August 24. On this important day for the Comintern, Fischer
visited Wilhelm Pieck and his family.

Wilhelm Pieck, who was then already sixty-three years old,
was not only the chairman of the German Communist party in
Moscow but a member of the ECCI. In 1931, he was appointed
a member of the ECCI Presidium and the ECCI Secretariat and
was, therefore, one of the top members of the Comintern. Pieck
lived with his entire family in Moscow: his son Arthur, Arthur's
wife Grete Lohde, and his daughter Elli Pieck Winter, who
worked as her father's secretary:

> Grete Lohde was the first in the Comintern to ask: "What
> do you think?" Once a German working class girl and now
> the daughter-in-law of the Chairman of the CP Germany, Grete
> was intelligent, conscientious, industrious and charming. She
> worked on the editorial staff of the journal *Communist Inter-
> national*. I liked her and cautiously helped to broaden her
> horizon and improve her ability to debate and to express
> herself. Unfortunately she had tuberculosis. Her eyes revealed
> that she was perplexed.
>
> I had been prepared by my talk with Gottwald and had
> thought about the pact, but was still in a state of shock. And
> yet I thought that the pact was good. "It's . . . it's—"
>
> "Treason? No. Dreadful? Yes," said Grete.

"We German comrades will never understand it. My father doesn't understand it either," said Elli Winter, who also worked as an editorial secretary.

"Neither does Arthur," said Grete. "No one understands it."

I tried to articulate the results of my reflections and justify the inevitability of the pact.

An hour later, Wilhelm Pieck telephoned Fischer to ask if he would be prepared to participate in a discussion with leading German Communists that evening in Pieck's country house in Kuntsevo.

Not only Pieck and his family were present but also Wilhelm Florin and Philip Dengel, two leaders of the CP Germany in Moscow. Other important members of the German party were also present, but Fischer could not recall exactly who. Ernst Fischer began with a somewhat lofty justification of the pact: Of course, it was disgraceful to applaud the pact with a joyous "yes"; Nazi Germany remained what it was, a country of concentration camps, mass murders, slaughter of the Jews, and a reign of terror. He argued that Hitler's temporary arrangement with Moscow neither changed him nor his system; but the pact enabled the Soviet Union to gain time, and the first thrust of the German war machine would not be against the USSR but against England and France. The Soviet Union needed time to regorganize its army so that it would be a match for the German Wehrmacht.

While I presented these arguments a sense of uneasiness began to rise in me and increased to the degree that I succeeded in convincing my interlocutors. My sense of reason was satisfied with itself, with its ability to come to terms with such a difficult situation. But that other feeling, where did it come from? Was it my double who had been suppressed? Were they moral reservations or the resistance of my conscience? Was I a Communist for whom the end justifies the means—the victory of the Soviet Union and therefore of Socialism—or was I a petit bourgeois intellectual who was afraid to soil his hands? I considered the pact reprehensible on moral grounds but necessary on political or even historical grounds; ergo it was my duty to convince others and myself. Why the devil did I have an uneasy feeling, a sense of antagonism between my conscience and my consciousness?

Fischer seemed to have convinced the guests, but there were a few questions.

"The decisive task of German Communists remains, therefore, the struggle against Hitler?"

"By all means," replied Fischer.

"But the pact!"

"The pact should not hinder us," replied Fischer. "Of course we cannot call for a revolutionary struggle while we're in Moscow. But we must emphasize that it is not the working class which has signed a pact with Hitler."

So much for Fischer's recollection of his discussion with leaders of the German Communist party on August 24, 1939. He later openly admitted that he had not recognized the central issue at that time. He made up for this in his memoirs, published in 1969.[11]

Ruth von Mayenburg: The Clock on the Kremlin Tower Stopped

Ruth von Mayenburg was born in Teplitz-Schönau in the Sudetenland in Czechoslovakia to prosperous parents. She became increasingly involved in leftist intellectual circles, and at the end of 1930 she met Ernst Fischer. Disappointed by the Social Democrats, von Mayenburg began to look toward the Soviet Union, attempting to understand and defend what was then called the Bolshevik experiment. In addition, she had personally experienced the menace of Fascism in Germany during a 1931 visit to Berlin with Fischer, whom she married in the summer of 1932. Von Mayenburg was deeply impressed by Dimitrov during the Reichstag fire trial in 1933. In February 1934, after the collapse of the Schutzbund uprising in Vienna, she joined the Austrian Communist party. Shortly thereafter, von Mayenburg emigrated to the Soviet Union, where she participated enthusiastically in the 1934 May Day celebration on Red Square. She began to work in the IV Division (military espionage) of the General Staff of the Red Army and traveled to Nazi Germany several times, under a pseudonym, on missions for the Soviet military. In the spring of 1937, von Mayenburg was relieved of her espionage activity after talking with Dimitrov and transferred to the Comintern.

She resided in the Hotel Lux with 600 other officials from practically every country. Her apartment was opposite that of the leader of the Spanish Communist party, Jesus Hernandez, and his wife Pilar. Then came the Hitler-Stalin pact:

> The Soviet Union concluded a non-aggression pact with Nazi Germany in August of 1939. It seemed to us as though the clock on the Kremlin tower stopped. Soon, however, the consternation which Stalin's "brilliant" move caused among anti-Fascists around the world—not only in the Soviet Union but beyond its borders—was replaced by a sense of *Realpolitik*: The homeland of socialism had to stay out of the war at any price.[12]

In a later interview, von Mayenburg clarified her views of 1939:

We were so shocked that we couldn't talk for a few hours. Then we began to ask one another: "What does it mean? Is it possible?" We talked about the Hitler-Stalin Pact and the fact that von Ribbentrop came to *them*. We knew nothing of the Secret Protocol; that was only revealed much later. However, even then there were rumors that the official non-aggression pact which was printed in the *Pravda* was not the only agreement. . . . In our minds we were Leninists, which is to say against imperialism, and countries such as England, America, and France were still imperialist countries. And so we tried to assuage our consciences by thinking about what the pact actually meant. The workers in Germany who opposed Hitler's regime, who were tortured and perished in the concentration camps—all that was called into question by the Hitler-Stalin Pact. They were suddenly victims who had perished for "higher" political considerations and without regard to what happened to Hitler's opponents in Germany. It was actually shameful, and we weren't able to overcome this feeling of shame for a long time. One had to mobilize one's Marxist concept of imperialism, of international struggles, of *everything*, in order to deceive oneself about this matter of conscience.[13]

Herbert Wehner also lived in the Hotel Lux, under the pseudonym Kurt Funk. Wehner, who was born in Dresden in 1906, joined the German Communist party in 1927 and was elected a Communist delegate to the parliament of Saxony in 1930. After Hitler seized power, Wehner joined the anti-Hitler resistance and was active in party affairs in Germany and abroad. In 1935, he emigrated to Prague and then to Moscow. In his memoirs, which were written in 1946 but not published until 1982, Wehner has only the following brief recollection of the pact: "The German-Soviet pact was the outward sign of a development which had been evident for some time. It was a tremendous burden for the German Communists in Moscow."[14]

The Head of the Communist Party
of New Zealand Traveling to Moscow

The head of the Communist party of New Zealand, Sidney
Wilfred Scott learned of the Hitler-Stalin pact in a most singular
manner—in a sleeping car from Leningrad to Moscow. Scott,
who was then thirty-nine years old, had, together with others,
founded the CP of New Zealand in April of 1921. He had been
editor-in-chief of that party's newspaper, the *Workers Weekly*,
for many years and, at the beginning of the 1930s, became the
party's director of propaganda.

In the early summer of 1939, Scott began a long trip. He
journeyed to Australia and then by ship to Southhampton, England, with stops in Colombo, Aden, Suez, and Malta. In London
he had extensive meetings with Harry Pollitt, the chairman of
the British Communist party, who tactfully explained some of
the problems in the Soviet Union. However, against Pollitt's
advice, Scott traveled to Leningrad aboard the Soviet ship *Koop-
eratsky*. He was greeted by the Comintern official Springhall: "I
rather liked him," Scott wrote, "but it became apparent that he
had become somewhat corrupted by his life as an official."

With Springhall's help, Scott found a room in a Leningrad
hotel. The following evening both took the night train to Moscow.
In their sleeping compartment Springhall and Scott began to
talk:

> At one of the stations he [Springhall] managed to find a news-
> paper and opening it, he suddenly became excited. "Listen
> to this, Scott," he said, and translating from the Russian he
> read out an announcement to the effect that Russia and Ger-
> many had signed a pact of non-aggression and amity. To say
> that I was surprised is an understatement. Its implications,
> or some of them, were obvious enough. I did not hesitate to
> express my consternation and criticized the Soviet govern-

ment's action. But Springhall interrupted me, saying sternly that one must never criticize the Soviet government. It was the fatherland of the workers and was never wrong.[15]

Scott later justified the pact with the usual arguments that all attempts to reach an agreement with the Western powers had failed and that the Soviet leadership was left with practically no other alternative. It was only many years later that he concluded that the pact with Hitler had been signed to enable the Soviet Union to annex territories in Eastern Europe.

An Official of the Central Committee of the CPSU Speaks to the Comintern

Enrique Castro Delgado and all of the other officials of the Comintern had been told that at 6:00 P.M. on August 24, a representative of the Central Committee of the CPSU would speak on the "international situation." Everyone arrived punctually to hear such an important speech. The only record of this meeting is found in Delgado's memoirs. His recollections may be excessively ironic, but, as anyone who has witnessed similar meetings in Moscow knows, they probably describe the event reasonably accurately. Here is Delgado's description of the speech:

> Dimitrov, Manuilski, Marty, Togliatti, Pieck, Florin, Gottwald and several other important officials, including the speaker, were on the platform. Vilkov, the Secretary of the Comintern's Party organization rose with a paper in his hand. . . .
>
> "Comrades, we begin by nominating the honorary presidium." There is a pause.

Vilkov: "Comrade Stalin." . . . We stand and applaud wildly.

Vilkov: "Comrade Molotov." . . . We rise and applaud a little less.

Vilkov: "Comrade Voroshilov." . . . We stand and applaud as we did for Molotov, then sit down.

Vilkov: "Comrade Kalinin." . . . We rise and applaud slightly less than for Molotov and Voroshilov.

Vilkov: "Comrade Andreyev." . . . We stand, applaud as for Kalinin and sit down.

Vilkov: "Comrade Kaganovich." . . . We rise, applaud somewhat less and take our seats.

Vilkov: "Comrade Mikoyan." . . . We stand, applaud somewhat less and sit down.

Vilkov: "Comrade Khrushchev." . . . We rise, applaud as for Mikoyan, and take our seats.

Vilkov: "Comrade Beria." . . . We stand, applaud madly and sit down.

Vilkov: "Comrade Shvernik." . . . We rise, applaud a little and take our seats. And so we elect our honorary presidium. I breathe deeply, wipe my brow and prepare to hear the speaker. However Vilkov waves yet another piece of paper in his hand: "Comrades, we will now appoint the working presidium." I clench my teeth. I think that the others do too. And so the same voice that already announced ten names continues tirelessly and pitilessly on, as though there were not enough of them, they who formed the most glorious leadership of the most glorious party.

"Comrade Dimitrov.". . . We rise, applaud and sit down.

"Comrade Manuilski." . . . We rise, applaud and sit down.

"Comrades Blagoeva, Belov, Stepanov." . . . We remain in our seats and do not applaud. We are somewhat tired and our hands hurt a bit. But it was worth the trouble, for we have two presdiums: an honorary presdium and a working presidium.

The speaker does what speakers around the world do: he

goes to the podium, shuffles his papers, looks to see if he has the obligatory glass of water (in Moscow it's tea), passes his hand across his forehead as though he had to reflect about what he was about to say, looks at the audience, clears his throat and begins: "Comrades . . ."

Ten minutes pass.

". . . Comrade Stalin, who foresaw the danger . . ."

Applause prevents the speaker from finishing his sentence, if it was ever meant to be finished. The speaker smiles and smiles.

Twenty minutes pass.

The speaker stares at the audience. I think that he is looking at me, and I look away. He pauses and continues: "The imperialists wanted to direct the German army to the East . . . but the perspicacity of our brilliant helmsman, Comrade Stalin." . . . Again thundering applause. Thirty minutes pass, forty minutes pass. We have applauded stormily four times. Fifty minutes pass. One hour. We have applauded stormily six times. The speaker has no more tea in his glass and only a few sheets of paper left to read.

Many of those in the audience do not seem to be listening; some in my row have a newspaper spread on their knees so that those on the platform cannot see that they're reading. It seems that others are sleeping with their eyes open—Dimitrov doodles for a long time on a few sheets of paper; when one sheet is full he crumples it and places it carefully before him. Manuilski is extremely occupied with his old pipe; it appears that he succeeded in cleaning it after much effort. The other members of the presidium appear to be listening as though enchanted.

At last the speaker is holding the last sheet of paper. ". . . and the criminal ploy engineered by the imperialist dogs was foiled thanks to this pact of immeasurable historical significance, the expression of the political genius of our comrade Stalin." The presidium rises to its feet. We too stand. The presidium applauds and we applaud. The last storm of applause begins to die down. Dimitrov takes his seat. Manuilski takes his seat. We take our seats. The speaker gathers his papers, looks for his glass of tea, takes out a handkerchief, wipes his brow, leaves the podium and sits down next to the presidium. I wait. Vilkov rises. I shudder. It seems as though even the columns shudder: "Comrades: In the name of the presidium I would like to suggest that we send a resolution to Comrade Stalin . . ." He reads. I listen without understanding. We all rise and applaud. I too applaud. We approve of the non-aggression pact.

Vilkov: "The meeting is adjourned."

We begin to leave the hall. The human stream divides to let the presidium pass. At the end of the presidium is the speaker who smiles at everyone. I look at him and smile. It is all like a meeting of the *Pravda*.[16]

Excursus: Many Secrets and No Directives

The previous recollections of leading Comintern officials reveal four significant facts:

1. *Secrecy*. Very few people in the Soviet Union were aware of the preparations for the Hitler-Stalin pact; in the Soviet government apparently only Stalin and Molotov were informed. As Khrushchev's memoirs make clear, even some members of the Soviet Politburo were not informed: Stalin simply let them go hunting. The same is true of the leadership of the Comintern: even such important figures as Wilhelm Pieck and Jesus Hernandez—both of whom were members of the highest bodies of the Executive Committee—only heard of the pact on the radio or read about it in the newspaper. Although we may assume that the General Secretary of the Comintern, Dimitrov, was informed, no one can be certain

because none of those who recalled the pact in their memoirs
mentions talking with Dimitrov. Dimitrij Manuilski was certainly aware that the pact was being prepared, and Ernst
Fischer's memoirs show that Klement Gottwald, the Secretary
of the Czechoslovak CP and the Comintern Secretary for Central Europe, was also apparently cognizant.

2. *The pact and the partition of Poland*. Well-informed
observers always viewed the pact in connection with the imminent partition of Poland. This is apparent in Gottwald's
discussion with Ernst Fischer on August 21 and in Manuilski's
meeting with Jesus Hernandez after the signing. The connection between the pact and the imminent partition of Poland
between Nazi Germany and the Soviet Union is significant
and should be noted.

3. *Official organizations not convoked*. Contrary to standard procedure, neither the ECCI (the expanded Executive
Committee) of the Comintern nor the two smaller but more
important bodies, the ECCI Presidium and the ECCI Secretariat, were convoked. Instead, there was only a speech delivered by a representative of the Soviet Central Committee,
which made clear how little respect Stalin apparently had for
the Comintern.

4. *Lack of directives*. Neither immediately before the signing of the pact nor in the days and weeks after the pact was
signed did the heads of the Communist International inform
the leaders of the various national Communist parties. In the
decisive weeks following the signing of the pact, no official
statements—or even internal instructions—from the Comintern leaders were issued to the leaders of the other national
Communist parties. Even the official history, *The Communist
International—A Short Historical Outline*, does not mention
a directive from the Comintern to the Communist leaders in
other countries.

The lack of such a directive is indeed astounding; the Comintern always issued directives, instructions, and advice even about minor issues—but said nothing about such a major turning point! The Comintern leaders, otherwise so eager to instruct, veiled themselves in secrecy. Why?

There are two possible answers. The first is that Stalin disregarded or even disdained the Comintern, which he had once referred to as a *lavochka* or "little shop." Perhaps he used the decisive event of August 23, 1939, to express his disdain.

The second possibility is that Stalin wanted to test the leaders of the Communist parties in other countries to determine whether or not they would loyally support the Soviet leaders and defend Soviet policies, even when confronted with a shift that seemed incredible. Perhaps, Stalin wanted to see how the leaders of other Communist parties would react under these circumstances and thereby learn whose unswerving loyalty he could count on no matter what happened.

The Concern of the German Ambassador von der Schulenburg

In addition to the reactions of the Comintern officials, it seems necessary to mention the impressions of certain foreign ambassadors in Moscow who had an intimate knowledge of Soviet politics and who had direct contact with the Soviet Union and its leaders. Among these was the German Ambassador to Moscow, Friedrich Werner Graf von der Schulenburg (1875–1944), who joined the German diplomatic corps in 1901. In 1923 he was appointed envoy to Teheran and from 1931–1934 to Bucharest. As Ambassador to Moscow from 1934 until 1941, he was actively involved in preparing the Hitler-Stalin pact, albeit against his will. Von der Schulenburg was extremely critical of the Nazi regime. The anti-Nazi resistance planned to appoint him foreign minister in a government headed by Goerdeler. Von der Schulenburg was condemned to death after the anti-Hitler coup failed on July 20, 1944, and was executed in the Berlin-Plötzensee prison on November 10 of the same year.

Hans von Herwarth, who was on friendly terms with Ambassador von der Schulenburg, was aware of his concerns. At the beginning of 1939 it became clear that Schulenburg's ideas about improving German-Soviet relations were completely contradictory to Hitler's. Von Herwarth recorded that "Schulenburg's goal was to reestablish the previous good relations with the USSR, whereas Hitler wanted to buy Stalin's consent to Hitler's invasion of Poland with a treaty with the Soviet Union."[17]

Now the Hitler-Stalin pact had been signed. Von Herwarth recorded his meeting with the ambassador on the morning of August 24: "On the morning of August 24 Schulenburg was, contrary to his usual habit, already in his office at 9:00." Schulenburg openly expressed his concern to von Herwarth about the impending war, which, after the conclusion of the Hitler-Stalin pact, had now become inevitable: "This war will, like the First World War, last a long, long, time," thought Schulenburg and added: "I have worked with all my strength to establish good relations between Germany and the Soviet Union and have, to a certain degree, attained my goal. However you know yourself that in reality I have achieved nothing. This treaty will bring us the Second World War and destroy Germany."

Herwarth saw von der Schulenburg's personal tragedy in the fact that he had to participate in this development.[18]

Paasikivi and Gafencu on the Pact

In addition to the remarks of Ambassador von der Schulenburg, there is interest in the reminiscences of two diplomats who were very closely involved with the Soviet Union for many years, and who left important comments on the pact based on their intimate knowledge and experience—the Finn, Juho Kusti Paasikivi and the Rumanian, Grigore Gafencu.

Paasikivi (1870–1956) studied history and law in Helsinki and in 1918 became a member of the first free Finnish government. He spoke Russian fluently and in 1920 negotiated a peace treaty with Soviet leaders in Tartu. Although his views were, on the whole, conservative, he adhered to the group known as the "Old Finns," who opposed Finnish nationalism and chauvinism and who advocated a compromise with the Soviet Union. From 1936 until 1939, Paasikivi was the Finnish envoy to Stockholm, where he heard about the Hitler-Stalin pact, and from September 1939 until 1940 he directed the Finnish negotiations in Moscow, where he frequently met with Stalin and Molotov. Paasikivi was the Prime Minister of Finland from November 1944 until March 1946 and President from 1945 to 1956. In his memoirs, which were published in the 1960s, Paasikivi maintained that the preconditions for a pact between the USSR and Nazi Germany were the internal transformation of the Soviet Union and its desire to consider itself a great power. By the mid-1930s the Soviet empire had, in the course of the five-year plans, developed its economy, particularly its heavy industry—which was the foundation of its military potential—and reorganized its army. In Paasikivi's opinion, these changes had political and psychological effects on the country.

The self-confidence of the rulers in the Kremlin and of the Russian people as well as the proud consciousness of their

own strength as a great power increased. . . . Communist
ideology was increasingly accompanied by Russian patriotism. . . . In the 1930s Soviet-Russian nationalism and patriotism was expressed more and more frequently. Soviet
Russia's period of weakness was over . . . Russian imperialism, which had been dormant until then, awoke and came
to life. The feeling of strength and importance, of initiative
and size became stronger. The door to Europe was opened for
the Soviet Union which was accepted as a great power and
an active participant in ordering European affairs.

To this were added certain similarities between the systems
in Nazi Germany and the Soviet Union, making it easier for
them to cooperate.[19]

The agreement of August 23, 1939, between Germany and
the Soviet Union and the agreement signed in Munich in the
autumn of 1938, would, in Paasikivi's opinion, "be considered
the most fateful and unfortunate acts of state in recent history."
At the beginning, the true nature of the agreement of 1939 was
not known, but within a few months it became apparent.

Although people suspected that secret clauses were appended to the Pact there were no details to that effect at the
time. However when Germany and the Soviet Union both
attacked Poland in September and divided it amongst themselves and when the Kremlin began its intensive activity
against the Baltic states and Finland as well as against Rumania in the summer of 1940 it became apparent that the
Ribbentrop-Molotov treaty had laid the foundation for this
development.[20]

The Rumanian Grigore Gafencu (1892–1957) also emphasized that the transformation of the Soviet system was a precondition for the Hitler-Stalin pact. Gafencu, who had been a

leading member of the National Peasants party in the 1920s, was elected a member of the Rumanian parliament in 1928. As Foreign Minister of Rumania from December 1939 to May 1940, he was concerned with maintaining Rumania's neutrality. He was the Rumanian ambassador to Moscow from August 1940 until June 1941. He opposed Antonescu's dictatorial regime in Rumania and the war, so he emigrated in 1944 to Switzerland, where he published his memoirs, *Prelude to the Russian Campaign*.

Like Paasikivi, Gafencu observed the revival of Russian nationalism, the emphasis on Soviet patriotism, and the reestablishment of military traditions—among them the obligation that soldiers salute one another on the street (which had been abolished in 1917), the reintroduction of ranks, and the glorification of military life.

Golden stars studded with precious stones glittered on the chests of the marshals, of a magnificence unknown to the ordinary citizen. These were only the outward signs of the gigantic effort imposed on all the financial and economic resources, all the forces of labour and production of the vast Empire, in hammering out the most formidable war machine that Russia has ever known.

Gafencu recognized that "the Moscow Pact was, in this sense, a piece of nationalistic policy." In Gafencu's opinion, Stalin sought refuge at a critical moment in nationalism and looked to it for support. "What does account for . . . the ease with which the terms of the Moscow agreement were resolved is not the similarity between the true sentiments of the two peoples, but the appearance of similitude in the outlook of the leaders of the two empires." Gafencu was struck by the number of aspects that the regimes of Hitler and Stalin had in common.

They showed the same authoritarian means of imposing the will of the ruler, without the possibility of reply; the same determination on the part of the master to hold the supreme authority against all comers; the same absence of control, criticism or any manifestation of an independent public opinion, a lack of control that assured to the dictator complete freedom of movement, and the possibility of justifying even the most outrageous change-about by clever propaganda; the same interest in bulk, the sole concern under a totalitarian policy: the same urge to organise, arm, motorise and mechanise ever greater and greater numbers ("Eighty million Germans," said one Berlin newspaper with ineffable pride the day after von Ribbentrop's visit to Moscow, "and a hundred and eighty million Russians. Their union represents a combination possessing the greatest military and industrial strength in the world, and an empire which stretches over Europe and Asia, far greater than the greatest mass of territory—*laendermasse*—that has ever existed"); the same disdain for the small states which could not, alone, defend their security, their neutrality or their existence; the same intention to absorb them in the vital space reserved for the imperial masses; the same bias towards simple geographical boundaries, boldly drawn and cutting neighboring countries into pieces; the same worship of strength.

Soviet militarism, at whose disposal were put labour and industrial production, the preparation of all citizens for battle, even down to the education of children, had little to learn from German militarism. It shared the same economic romanticism, the indulgence in wild dreams, in plans covering years and decades, schemes to harness the energies of rivers and tides, and to move mountains, the same urge to change the order of things and astound the gods—although the social concept and the creative spirit were essentially opposite.

Gafencu observed that "these political styles, so much alike, created a most favourable atmosphere for political collaboration in both Berlin and Moscow. . . . It appeared that the two regimes had suddenly realised their affinity, now that the curtain was drawn, and the profits that might accrue."[21]

After Six Days of Silence: The Supreme Soviet

Let us return to the Soviet Union in the first days after the signing of the pact. The pact was the focus of attention in the Soviet press for only two days. On August 24, the press published the photographs of Stalin and von Ribbentrop and of the Soviet and German leaders, the text of the agreement, and the previously mentioned editorial explaining the event. On the following day, the press published the communiqué about von Ribbentrop's departure. Thereafter, there was absolutely nothing about the pact; the agreement simply wasn't mentioned. The Soviet press returned as quickly as possible to business as usual—on August 25, the editorial in the *Pravda* discussed the government's purchases of vegetables.

The signing of the Hitler-Stalin pact was not followed by a meeting of the Central Committee as was usual on such important occasions. Neither the Central Committee nor the Ministry of Foreign Affairs published a statement. There were none of the usual "spontaneous" and "enthusiastic" factory meetings and demonstrations to explain such an important event. The Soviet press, presumably on Stalin's orders, did nothing to explain the pact to party members, Soviet officials, or the populace at large. "It was not till August 31—i.e., one day before the German invasion of Poland—that Molotov made a statement on the Soviet-German Pact before the Supreme Soviet."[22]

Both the Spanish Communist Enrique Castro Delgado, known

as Luis Garcia, and the Soviet naval officer N. G. Kuznetsov attended the meeting of the Supreme Soviet and recorded their impressions in their memoirs. Castro Delgado: "Today Blagoeva called me to her office and gave me a small red card: the invitation to the Kremlin. She advised me to have all of my personal documents with me. . . . Back in my office I turned the card over and over: the emblem of the USSR, several lines of printed text and two hand-written words which I assumed meant Luis Garcia."

Although he lived only 800 meters from the Kremlin, Delgado was afraid that he would arrive too late. He went quickly from the Hotel Lux across Gorky Street to Red Square. Did he have all the necessary papers with him? The invitation, the *propusk* ("entrance pass") of the Comintern, and his residence permit, which said that he was stateless. Well aware of the way things were done in the Soviet Union, he made sure that his pseudonym, Luis Garcia, was written in the same way on all of the documents.

He was first stopped before the Kremlin gate: two NKVD (secret police) officers compared the photographs in his papers with his face, and then examined the invitation, the entrance pass, and his passport. In those days the Kremlin was hermetically closed to the public; only those were admitted who had business there. Delgado noted the superbly kept gardens, the clean houses, and the guards in front of every building. "The atmosphere was like that of an old monastery; there was utter silence, only broken by our steps." Again there were two guards; finally he was in the large assembly hall. A man in civilian clothes approached him and showed him to his seat.

The high point of the meeting was, according to Delgado, not Molotov's speech, but Stalin's brief appearance. Delgado recalled:

More and more men mount the platform . . . the ovation is deafening . . . I applaud . . . it hurts but I continue to applaud.

Stalin!

I am only twenty meters away from him. Can you imagine what that means? My gaze doesn't stray, I stare at only one man: Stalin. The others put on their headphones—I put mine on too. The others listen to the man who began to speak; I only stare, not at the speaker but at the man seated behind the speaker.

I think that the German-Soviet treaty was approved. I, however, only saw Stalin. [23]

Although Delgado's attention was captured by Stalin's brief appearance, the People's Commissar for Foreign Affairs of the USSR, Vjaceslav Molotov, delivered an important speech which dealt with the Hitler-Stalin pact.

August 23 must be regarded as a date of great historic importance. It is a turning point in the history of Europe, and not only of Europe. Only recently the German Nazis conducted a foreign policy which was essentially hostile to the Soviet Union. Yet, until recently, in the realm of foreign policy, the Soviet Union and Germany were enemies. The situation has now changed, and we have stopped being enemies.

Molotov knew, of course, that war would break out in Europe shortly after the conclusion of the pact, but he attempted to play down the fact: "Even if a military collision cannot be avoided in Europe, the scale of such a war will be limited. Only the partisans of a general war in Europe can be dissatisfied with this."

For the first time, Molotov avoided criticizing Nazi Germany or Fascism; instead he vehemently attacked Western social dem-

ocrats who until then had been courted as friends and allies in
the Popular Front from 1936 until 1938. Now, however, Molotov
explained that

> The Soviet-German agreement has been violently attacked in
> the Anglo-French and American press, and especially in some
> "socialist" papers. . . . Particularly violent in their de-
> nunciations of the agreement are some of the French and
> British socialist leaders. . . . These people are determined
> that the Soviet Union should fight against Germany on the
> side of Britain and France. One may well wonder whether
> these warmongers haven't gone off their heads. (Laughter) . . .
> If these gentlemen have such an irresistible desire to go to
> war, well then—let them go to war by themselves, without
> the Soviet Union. (Laughter and cheers) We'll see what kind
> of warriors they will make. (Loud laughter and cheers).[24]

These passages of Molotov's speech have, needless to say,
not been mentioned in Soviet works on foreign affairs for many
years.

At the end of the meeting, Scerbakov, a member of the Politburo, delivered a speech. He attempted to demonstrate that
the British and French had not negotiated with the Soviet Union
in good faith. "He then proposed that, in view of the 'perfect
clarity' of Molotov's statement, there should be no debate, that
the policy of the Soviet government be approved and the Soviet-
German agreement ratified." The naval officer N. G. Kuznetsov
recalled this moment and the subsequent formal vote: "We, the
deputies of the Supreme Soviet, voted unanimously for the rat-
ification of the treaty."[25]

Only a few hours after the end of this meeting of the Supreme
Soviet, on the morning of September 1, 1939, German troops
attacked Poland. France and Great Britain responded by de-
claring war on Germany. The Second World War had begun.

The Secret Protocol

Despite the political and ideological landslide that it caused, the nonaggression pact was not the most important topic of the meeting between von Ribbentrop, Stalin, and Molotov during the evening of August 23, 1939; it was the Secret Protocol appended to the pact that delimited the Soviet and German spheres of interest in Eastern Europe. The text of this secret protocol follows:[26]

Secret Additional Protocol

On the occasion of the signature of the Non-Agression Pact between the German Reich and the Union of Soviet Socialist Republics the undersigned plenipotentiaries of each of the two parties discussed in strictly confidential conversations the question of the boundary of their respective spheres of influence in Eastern Europe. These conversations led to the following conclusions:

Article I. In the event of a territorial and political rearrangement in the areas belonging to the Baltic States (Finland, Estonia, Latvia, Lithuania), the northern boundary of Lithuania shall represent the boundary of the spheres of influence of Germany and the U.S.S.R. In this connection the interest of Lithuania in the Vilna area is recognized by each party.

Article II. In the event of a territorial and political rearrangement of the areas belonging to the Polish state, the spheres of influence of Germany and the U.S.S.R. shall be bounded approximately by the line of the rivers Narev, Vistula and San.

The question of whether the interests of both parties make desirable the maintenance of an independent Polish State and how such a state should be bounded can only be definitely determined in the course of further political developments.

In any event both Governments will resolve this question by means of a friendly agreement.

Article III. With regard to Southeastern Europe attention is called by the Soviet side to its interest in Bessarabia. The German side declares its complete political disinterestedness in these areas.

Article IV. This protocol shall be treated by both parties as strictly secret.

Moscow, August 23, 1939.

For the Government	Plenipotentiary of the
of the German Reich	Government of the U.S.S.R.
v. Ribbentrop	V. Molotov

According to this secret agreement, Lithuania fell within Germany's sphere of interest, while the two other Baltic republics, Estonia and Latvia, together with Finland fell within the Soviet sphere. Five weeks later, at the end of September 1939, the Secret Protocol was altered: Lithuania was considered within the Soviet sphere of interest, for which Germany received certain parts of Poland.

The fourth clause of the agreement—"This protocol shall be treated by both parties as strictly secret"—was observed to the letter. The fourteen members of the staff of the German Embassy in Moscow had to swear in writing to keep absolutely secret not only the contents of the agreement, which were known to only three or four of them anyway, but even the existence of a "certain secret protocol." This signed declaration was dated August 27, 1939, and placed in a sealed envelope.[27]

The Secret Protocol dividing Eastern Europe into spheres of influence only became known in the West after World War II. It soon became the subject of much discussion and analysis. In the Soviet Union, however, the Secret Protocol remained a secret for forty-nine years, from 1939 until 1988. Not even an indirect reference to the Secret Protocol could be included in lectures or publications until the ban was lifted in 1988. Scholarly studies published in the USSR about Soviet foreign policy or Soviet-German relations were forbidden to refer to the protocol in any way until 1988. Even during the period of de-Stalinization from 1956 until 1964, which the Soviet historian Alexander Nekrich called a period of "liberation from the burden of the past, years of creative surge," this taboo remained untouched. Born in Baku in 1920, Alexander Nekrich is Professor at the Institute of History of the Academy of Sciences of the USSR. Nekrich and the Director of the Historical Institute, V. M. Xvostov, wrote a book entitled *How World War II Occurred*, in which they said:

> Although the book was devoted to the origin of the Second World War we avoided a discussion of one of the most important questions: the role of the Soviet-German pact of 1939 in unleashing the war. This question was and is the most delicate point of Soviet historiography. None of the Soviet historians dared at that time to transgress the boundary of what was allowed. . . . Had we tried to do so our manuscript would never have been published.[28]

This was true, as mentioned previously, for the somewhat freer period during the "thaw" from 1956 to 1964. In the Brezhnev era, from October 1964 until November 1982, as well as during the brief tenures of Andropov and Chernenko, an open discussion of the Hitler-Stalin pact was unthinkable. During this period, the Secret Protocol that delimited the spheres of influence between Nazi Germany and the Soviet Union could neither be mentioned nor referred to indirectly. Only recently, after M. S. Gorbachev was appointed General Secretary of the CPSU in March 1985, has the Hitler-Stalin pact been discussed more openly; details are found in the introduction to this book.

All of the memoirs quoted in the next three chapters record the reactions of people during August and September of 1939, a time when the Secret Protocol was not known to the public. Their impressions are, therefore, based solely on the officially published text of the nonaggression pact.

2

THE PACT AND THE PEOPLE
IN THE SOVIET UNION

The Soviet populace reacted to the pact in many different ways: some were surprised, others were dismayed or anxious, while others reassured themselves that Stalin always knew best. However, we must remember that during the Stalin era, and especially after the Great Purge of 1936–1938, people were very wary of expressing an opinion. As a result, foreign correspondents had difficulty determining the reaction of the populace to the pact. On the one hand, the press emphasized the feeling of surprise or concern: "The Russians were thunderstruck and tried in vain to adapt to this change of events" wrote the *New York Times* on August 28, 1939. The British writer and historian Alexander Werth, who lived in the Soviet Union, concurred that "there was a great deal of uneasiness in the country."[1]

On the other hand, the *Manchester Guardian* wrote on August 25, 1939, that "there is no evidence that the well-disciplined Soviet population finds anything unpleasing in the reversal of Soviet foreign policy, in spite of the feverish propaganda for years past against the Fascist aggressors." The *Times* of London noted that the Soviet press began to deal with other topics shortly after the signing of the pact: "The newspapers this week-end treated the gravest national crisis in a detached and non-committal way. *Pravda*'s leading article was 'Vegetables'."[2]

Three Soviets Recall the Event

The memoirs of three Soviets record the mixed feelings felt by the Soviet populace upon learning of the pact. The first is that of Oksana Kasenkina, a teacher who suffered during the Stalinist purges and who later emigrated to New York. She recorded that "overnight the most hated enemy of the Soviet Union became its 'friend and ally.' It took a long time for the people to realize it was not a joke."[3]

The memoirs of Anatoli Granovski describe the atmosphere of mistrust, which was so pervasive that one was even afraid to say too much to one's friends. Granovski was trained in the 1930s in the Soviet air defense artillery, where he had many discussions, including critical ones, with his friend Alexander. Anatoli and Alexander also discussed the signing of the Hitler-Stalin pact, but each feared that the other would report his comments to the authorities. Granovski proceeded cautiously: "I do not believe that they (the Germans) are our friends as the newspapers say any more than you do. I wonder why the government tries to deceive us."

However, Alexander was afraid of entering into such a discussion: " 'It is very difficult to govern' he said. 'I think they know best what they are doing. Anyhow, the policy has been decided on by Stalin, and there is the end to it.' "[4]

M. I. Gallai was a student in August 1939 and later an officer in the Soviet armed forces. In an article published in the Soviet Union he recalled how confused he was after learning of the pact: "Many things seemed inexplicable, weird and unnatural.

It was not primarily the pact itself which evoked doubts. It was clear to everyone that, under the circumstances, there was no other choice. Most of us took the pact like bitter medicine— unpleasant but necessary." However, the "uneasy feeling" remained. Looking at the front page of the *Pravda* with the photos of the recent mortal enemies shaking hands made Gallai uneasy because "things which we had become accustomed to seeing as hostile, evil and dangerous in the Komsomol (the party's youth organization) and even in the Pioneers (the party's organization for children) had somehow suddenly become virtually neutral." And so the events surrounding the pact remained "strange and incomprehensible" to him.[5]

Discussions in the Industrial City Kemerovo

Viktor Kravchenko, who was thirty-four in 1939, has left us a relatively detailed portrait of his reaction. Kravchenko joined the Communist party in 1929; during the Great Purge and at the time of the Hitler-Stalin pact he was the director of a factory in the Siberian city of Kemerovo. In August of 1943, Kravchenko traveled as a member of a purchasing commission to the United States, where he defected in April 1944. His memoirs, entitled *I Chose Freedom*, published in 1946, describe how party members and engineers in Kemerovo reacted to the news of the pact:

It was at Kemerovo that I saw the pact streak meteorlike across our horizon and crash headlong into the minds and consciences of the Party membership. It left us all stunned, bewildered and groggy with disbelief. . . . We had so long taken it for granted that the Nazis had only one real enemy, the Soviet regime. . . . After all, hatred of Nazism had been drummed into our minds year after year. We had seen our

leading Army Generals, including Tukhachevsky, shot for
supposed plotting with Hitler's Reichswehr. The big treason
trials, in which Lenin's most intimate associates perished, had
rested on the premise that Nazi Germany and its Axis friends,
Italy and Japan, were preparing to attack us. . . . The villainy
of Hitler had become in our land almost as sacred an article
of faith as the virtue of Stalin. Our Soviet children played
games of Fascists and Communists; the Fascists, always given
German names, got the worst of it every time. . . . In the
shooting galleries the targets were often cut-outs of brown-
shirted Nazis flaunting Swastikas. . . . Not until we saw news-
reels and newspaper pictures showing a smiling Stalin shaking
hands with von Ribbentrop did we begin to credit the incredible. The swastika and the hammer-and-sickle flying side
by side in Moscow!

As great as the shock and consternation at the signing of the
pact were, the populace still began to quickly seek some sort
of justification. The simplest, and therefore the most acceptable,
justification was that the Soviet leadership knew best of all what
had to be done. Nevertheless, there was no enthusiasm for the
new policy—on the contrary, the people were embarrassed and
reserved, as Kravchenko recalled:

> We discussed the new turn of events not only at formal
> meetings of the Party cells, but also privately, in our own
> homes and offices. How can we people in Kemerovo, we said
> or implied, pretend to understand such grave matters? Our
> job was to build and run factories, and to govern the people
> working in the factories, secure in the faith that our Beloved
> Leader could make no mistakes. Only a recalcitrant few among
> the Party people, indeed, continued to think about the matter
> at all. The rest were soon as apathetic as the population at
> large. After twenty-two years of life under a dictatorship,
> genuine public opinion had become unthinkable. . . .

Though everyone accepted the new friendship with the Nazis, along with the mounting attacks on other European countries, I can attest that there was nowhere any enthusiasm for these things. The whole business was edged with embarrassment. Our political meetings, at which speakers from the center explained the new situation, seemed constrained and fidgety.[6]

Leningrad: Leopold Grünwald and Li-tung Justify the Pact

The regional committee of the Leningrad party organization invited foreign communists to explain and justify the Hitler-Stalin pact at party meetings, apparently on the assumption that Soviet citizens would be more convinced than if they only heard Soviet speakers. Leopold Grünwald, who was born in Vienna, participated in one of these meetings. Grünwald was one of the cofounders of the Austrian Communist party in 1918, and several years later one of the cofounders of the Czech CP. Although he was often in Germany and Austria, he was primarily occupied during the 1920s in the German section of the Czech CP, especially in the German-speaking Sudetenland. After the German occupation of Czechoslovakia in March 1939, he fled to the Soviet Union. He was asked to speak on the Hitler-Stalin pact at a meeting of the Leningrad party on September 1, 1939. He recalled the following:

Exactly on September 1, 1939, the day war was declared, I started a ten-day lecture tour to Leningrad together with my Chinese friend Li-tung. We held meetings every day in large factories and offices and had one major duty: to present arguments for the shift of Soviet policy which led to the Hitler-Stalin Pact. When we received letters of thanks from the

Leningrad Lecturers for Public Education, signed by the members of the Regional Committee Chockrakov and Shamov together with flowers and gifts we felt uneasy.

Grünwald had accepted the nonaggression pact of August 23 without significant pangs of conscience. However, even he was critical of the second German-Soviet treaty governing their common borders and "friendship," which was signed on September 28, 1939, after von Ribbentrop's second visit to Moscow. This second treaty included an even more far-reaching secret protocol than the first. At this time, Grünwald had begun to work in the Comintern building in Rostokino.

On my desk lay the *Pravda* with a photograph of the signing of a new agreement. It showed Molotov and von Ribbentrop who this time were signing a German-Soviet friendship treaty! Like most of my comrades I asked myself: was there really no other way? Even at that time some of the comrades objected that the Soviet government could have simply declared itself neutral in order to keep the USSR out of the impending war instead of concluding a friendship treaty with the mortal enemy of socialism and peace.

We did not know how wide-ranging the pact was. Only later did the contents of the "Border and Friendship Treaty," the addendum to the original non-aggression pact, reach us: Stalin and Hitler delimited their "spheres of interest in Eastern Europe." Lenin had called such secret treaties "agreements between robbers behind the people's back."[7]

Author's Recollection of August 23 in Yeysk

I too was in the Soviet Union at the time, and it may be of value to recall how my friends and I reacted to the signing of the

Hitler-Stalin pact. In those days, I lived in Children's Home No. 6 for the children of the members of the Austrian "Schutzbund" and for the children of German political emigrants in Moscow. By the summer of 1939, the Children's Home No. 6 on Kalashny Lane No. 12 was no longer a home for children, because we were all between seventeen and nineteen years old. In actuality, the home had been transformed into a sort of youth hostel for emigrants.

In our first years there we were privileged: Our clothes were sewn in special tailor shops; we had an Austrian cook and our own bus to transport us to and from school; the home had its own infirmary, directed by a German doctor. We received frequent invitations, were greeted with particular warmth, and were given as many tickets to the opera, operetta, and theater as we wanted. We were visited by German anti-Fascist writers, foreign delegations, and officials of the Austrian and German sections of the Comintern—for example, by Koplenig, who was then the General Secretary of the Austrian CP, or by Wilhelm Pieck. However, the residents of Children's Home No. 6 were not spared the terror of the Great Purge of 1936–1938: The parents of more and more children were arrested—including my own mother, who was sent to the Vorkuta labor camp in the Arctic Circle in September 1936. Even the teachers in the Karl Liebknecht School were arrested one after the other; and by 1937, we had to attend a Russian school. Even some in the home were arrested. The first was our instructor, the Austrian Communist Karl Zehetner, and later even one of the "children," the seventeen-year-old Rolf Geissler.

The purge ended at the beginning of 1939, and we all looked forward to a better and calmer future. The pupils of Home No. 6 were to spend the summer vacation of 1939 in different places in the southern Soviet Union. Ten or twelve of us, including me, were sent to Yeysk on the Sea of Azov as guests of a large military academy. Yeysk was a garrison town, where civilians were rarely seen. There were men in uniform everywhere with letters on their caps reading "V.M.A.U. imeni STALINA." This mysterious abbreviation stood for the Russian equivalent of Naval Air War College. It must have been an exceptionally big school, for the entire town seemed to consist of officers and naval airmen of the V.M.A.U.

We had been allotted a single building some distance from the town. The building was fine, but not right on the sea; however, the V.M.A.U. supplied a bus to take us to the sea every day and bring us back in the evening. After the gruesome years of the purge, these holidays were particularly wonderful. We were enjoying our first real rest although even here we were not entirely out of touch with ordinary life. During our holiday we were preparing ourselves for entry into the Komsomol, the Communist youth organization, which was soon to come. Every other afternoon, we had a session with our political director, Igor Speransky, for political education. As a matter of course, our studies centered on the *Short History of the Communist Party of the Soviet Union*, known as the "Short Course."

In mid-August we were invited to a ceremony at the Palace of Culture of the V.M.A.U. The lecture on international affairs was devoted to the usual bitter attack on Fascism and Nazi Germany, and the speaker did not miss the opportunity to add: "Comrades, men and women, we have here in this hall some of our foreign guests, the children of the German and Austrian anti-Fascists who took part in the struggle against the hideous dictatorship of Hitler." Every head then turned toward us, and after that we became well known all over the town of Yeysk and had a wonderful time. Our hosts visited us frequently to ask whether everything was to our liking. We found as much attention paid to us as in the early days in the Children's Home.

Three days later, our political director, Igor Speransky, was summoned into town at midday. "Just go and have your swim," he said. "I shall be back in the evening—I've been summoned into town."

"What's up then?"

"I've no idea, but it can hardly be anything important."

We went off happy and contented, to have our swim. We had hardly returned when suddenly our political director burst in in a state of great excitement: "Here's something really important," he shouted breathlessly. "I've got hold of a galley proof of to-morrow morning's paper in Yeysk."

"What's the news?" we all asked in chorus.

"We've just signed a nonaggression pact with Germany!" We stared at him open-mouthed. This was the last thing we could have expected. We had naturally been following the press closely, and we had assumed confidently that, in spite of all difficulties encountered during the negotiations, the Soviet Union, France, and England would soon conclude a treaty against the Fascist aggressors.

Our political director read out to us in solemn, official tones the announcement of the pact between the Soviet Union and Nazi Germany. From the first few sentences we still assumed that the substance of the treaty was no more than an obligation on each side to refrain from aggression. But then our political director read out the later articles of the treaty, and we listened dumbfounded. This was not simply a nonaggression pact; this was a complete reversal of the whole foreign policy of the Soviet Union. What could be the meaning of "keeping each other informed" about interests which the Soviet Union had in common with Hitler's government? Or of not joining any group of powers directed against Nazi Germany? It could mean only one thing —the complete abandonment of the struggle against Fascist aggression in all its forms!

We were thunderstruck. We sat there bewildered and silent.

Finally, Egon Dirnbacher, the youngest among us, said sadly, "Ah, what a pity, now we shall certainly never be allowed to see Charlie Chaplain in 'The Great Dictator'!" Young Egon had certainly understood the situation correctly. For in fact, as we were to see in a few days, the conclusion of the pact had an immediate effect on the internal political situation. For the present, it was impossible to continue the discussion, since nobody—not even our political director—could offer any explanation of the pact.

"Tomorrow morning there are certain to be exhaustive comments in the press," he said, to calm our excitement. "Besides, tomorrow I am going to visit the party headquarters in Yeysk. After that I shall be able to give you more detailed information, and tomorrow evening we shall be able to talk the whole thing over more fully." But this was never to come about.

The Home Is Closed

The following morning, the first day after the conclusion of the pact, we were awakened very early by our political director: "I've just had a telegram from Moscow. We're to return at once."

Troubled speculations absorbed us on the train to Moscow. What could be the significance of this sudden return? What effect would the conclusion of the pact have on our personal lives? At the train station we were met by some of the pupils of the Children's Home, who had spent their holidays at other resorts and had returned before us. "The Home has been closed!" they shouted at us.

It was the most shattering piece of news I could possibly have heard. The Home was everything in the world for us—it was where we lived, it was our life, our shield, our friend. And now it was gone forever. We were standing suddenly on the brink of a void, and life henceforth was impossible to envision.

"What will become of us now?"

"We've no more idea than you. Everything is going to be decided this afternoon."

With heavy hearts, we returned from the station to our Home at No. 12 Kalashny Lane. The scene there was like the aftermath of a battle. Furniture movers, painters, and plumbers were running about the house and packing things away. All our possessions had been put together in a single room. Some of the pupils had already packed their things and were ready to move, but they had no idea where to go. Others were running around the house—for so many years our home—in a state of bewilderment and despair.

Some meetings had been held, but no one knew what was to become of us. In reply to our questions, the teachers shrugged their shoulders and said, "We have no more idea than you have. The headmaster has gone to a conference."

After his return, there was a shout of "all of you into the big hall—the meeting's just going to begin!" In contrast to all our previous meetings, this one could hardly be described as formal. We sat on boxes or sacks or leaned against the walls. As usual, the proceedings began with a political introduction. Our headmaster explained the pact to us, drawing particular attention to the fact that the Western powers had refused to negotiate with the USSR on the basis of equality. They had intended to make use of the the Soviet Union to fight for the interests of the Western imperialist powers, but the great Stalin had seen through their game. The immediate conclusion of a pact with Germany had provided the conditions necessary for the Soviet Union to continue to live in peace and build up its power.

He then went on to speak of our home: "In the context of the new requirements of foreign policy, we too shall have to do some reorganization." By the phrase "some reorganization" we were to understand the immediate closing of our home. The new lines of policy were then announced by the headmaster in brief, cold, and unemotional tones. Clearly, no more trouble was to be taken to make the transition to the new situation easier for us to bear. Instinctively, I had the impression that we had already been written off.

Within half an hour, the whole thing was decided. The majority of the pupils were to be transferred that afternoon to the Spartacus Children's Home; the seniors, however, were to work in a factory, which would provide them with accommodations. That afternoon, forty of us were sent to the Spartacus home, where we were greeted with a cry of "everyone into the hall at once!" We stood disconsolately in the hall until a large, severe-looking, black-haired man came in and shouted out crossly, "Get into line!" This was not the tone of voice to which we were accustomed in our previous home, but we reluctantly obeyed.

Orders now began to shower down on us like a rain of blows: "No one is allowed to leave the home without the permission of one of the masters. All exercises will be done under the supervision of one of the masters. Everyone must conform to the established rules of the home." We were then shown where we were to sleep. We were horrified when we saw the dormitory with its primitive beds standing packed together in rows. After that came the evening meal—it goes without saying that it was inedible. The difference between this and our previous home was appalling. A heretical thought passed through my mind: "There will certainly be no foreign delegations visiting us here!"

The conclusion of a nonaggression pact with Nazi Germany and the closing of our home had transformed us overnight into ordinary Soviet citizens. It seemed barely credible that only two weeks before we had been traveling to the sea in a special bus provided by the military academy, or been treated as honored guests at a party given by hundreds of officers.[8]

The Transformation of Soviet Propaganda

The sudden, total shift in emphasis of Soviet propaganda immediately following the conclusion of the Hitler-Stalin pact left a strong and lasting impression on the Soviet populace. Viktor Kravchenko, a party member and the director of a factory in the Siberian city of Kemerovo, recalled:

Voks, the Society for Cultural Relations with Foreign Countries, instantly discovered the wonders of German *Kultur*. . . . The theaters of the capital were developing a great interest in German drama. In fact, everything Germanic was the vogue. A brutal John Bull and an Uncle Sam enthroned on money bags figured in the propaganda, but the Nazis were exempt from such ridicule.[9]

My own experience in Moscow confirmed this view. I too noted that attacks on and even criticism of Nazi Germany and Fascism disappeared over night. In fact, it seemed as though Fascism had never existed. Instead there was increasing criticism of "imperialism," which was either overtly stated or implied to mean Anglo-French imperialism.

The new foreign policy was clearly reflected in an immediate change in the cinema and, shortly thereafter, in the theater repertory. Already, on the evening of August 24, two anti-Fascist films, "Professor Mamlock," based on a play by Friedrich Wolf, and "The Oppenheim Family," based on a novel by Lion Feuchtwanger, were removed from cinemas all over the USSR. Theaters ceased to perform plays with an anti-Fascist message, including the play "The Sailors of Cattaro," even though it was about a sailors' rebellion in 1918 against the Austro-Hungarian monarchy. However, the censor probably thought that he could hardly be too careful about such a matter.

The change also affected the libraries. I used to visit the Library for Foreign Literature in Stoleshnikov Lane several times a week. It was located in a small church which had been closed after the revolution. I read the books of anti-Fascist writers, especially those of German writers who had emigrated from Germany. Only a few days after the pact, I found that a number of books by anti-Fascist authors were no longer available.[10]

Enrique Castro Delgado, who was still working in the Comintern, noted the change in propaganda: "Since August 24 things have changed greatly. German Fascism is neither referred to in the daily newspapers nor in magazines. Nor is it mentioned in the Comintern. The basis of the pact is, among other things, loyalty and in the name of this loyalty we 'temporarily forgot' German Fascism."[11]

A Change of Sentiment in the Soviet Populace

The Second World War began with Hitler's attack on Poland on September 1, 1939, and Britain's and France's declaration of war on Germany. Although official Soviet policy declared that the war was being waged by imperialists on both sides and that the Soviet Union was neutral, it was not difficult to see that the Soviet press was well disposed to the German cause. Both Radio Moscow and the Soviet press published the reports of the Wehrmacht first and the French and British communiqués second. The *Pravda* devoted more space to Hitler's speeches than to Churchill's. The slightest criticism of Nazi Germany was taboo, whereas the propaganda campaign against the British and French imperialists increased.[12]

This change of heart resulted in German Communist emigrants in the Soviet Union being treated better than those from other countries because they were German. Herbert Wehner, a leader of the German Communist party in emigration, who worked in the Comintern and lived in the Hotel Lux, provides a number of interesting examples of this phenomenon. Wehner recalled that an older German Communist, with whom he frequently spoke, recounted the following unusual incident shortly after the signing of the Hitler-Stalin pact. The German Communist was suddenly greeted and congratulated by the party secretary in the factory where he worked, even though the secretary had paid no special attention to him until then. The German emigrant asked with surprise for what he was being congratulated. "Why, for the success of the German troops in Poland," replied the party secretary.

"That's not a reason to congratulate me," replied the German Communist. The Soviet party official was surprised: "Does that mean that you don't want the Germans to beat the Poles?" The German Communist tried to explain: "I'm for the victory of the Revolution, not for the victory of Hitler." The party official, irritated, shook his head: "That's only rhetoric. Hitler is helping us with his victories over the Polish *pans* ('the great landowners')."

Another friend of Herbert Wehner, who was also a German Communist and who had spent several years in prison under the Nazis before emigrating, heard some of the passengers on a Moscow bus react to the latest newspaper reports on German victories in Poland by saying "Hitler *molodec!*" which means "Hitler is a fine fellow!"

This of course not only reflected popular sentiment but also official policy in the press. Whereas the Soviet press found ample

space for news about Nazi Germany and the press releases of
the German information service (Deutsche Nachrichtenbüro),
there was not the slightest reference to the death or burial of
the German Communist C. Wurm. As Herbert Wehner recalled,
everything was organized so as to forget that there were German
refugees in the Soviet Union.[13]

The Effect of Molotov's Speech
of October 31, 1939

After the Soviet invasion of Poland on September 17, 1939, the
annexation of Eastern Poland, and the second pact between Nazi
Germany and the Soviet Union governing "common borders and
friendship," Molotov delivered a speech before the Supreme
Soviet on October 31, 1939, which revealed that Soviet foreign
policy would be even more favorable to Nazi Germany. The
following is one of the most important parts of Molotov's speech,
which is never quoted in Soviet publications.

First of all, Molotov explained that

> the whole concept of "aggression" has changed. Today we
> cannot use the word in the same sense as three or four months
> ago. Now Germany stands for peace, while Britain and France
> are in favour of continuing the war. As you see, the roles have
> been reversed. Now Britain and France, no longer able to
> fight for a restoration of Poland, are posing as "fighters for
> democratic rights against Hilterism." The British Government
> now claims that its aim is, no more, or no less, if you please,
> "the destruction of Hitlerism." So it's an ideological war, a
> kind of medieval religious war. One may like or dislike Hit-
> lerism, but every sane person will understand that ideology
> cannot be destroyed by force. It is therefore not only non-
> sensical but also criminal to pursue a war "for the destruction

of Hitlerism" under the bogus banner of the struggle for democracy.[14]

Soviet propaganda was transformed even further after Molotov's speech. I found to my amazement that the emigre newspaper had disappeared from the Library for Foreign Literature and that they had been replaced by Nazi publications![15] According to the Comintern official Josef Berger, even prisoners in the labor camps noticed the change. Berger was one of the founders of the Communist party of Palestine in 1922 and later its secretary. In the late 1920s, he was responsible in the Comintern for the Near East and was active in Berlin as the Secretary of the Anti-Imperialist League. In 1932, he became Director of the Near Eastern Department of the Comintern in Moscow, was arrested during the Great Purge, and was in the Solovki labor camp at the time of the Hitler-Stalin pact.

According to Berger, the prisoners noticed that "the word 'Fascist' vanished from the papers. . . . Instead, the Nazis were respectfully referred to as the NSDAP (Nazional-sozialistische deutsche Arbeiterpartei), while their enemies were described as the 'Anglo-French capitalists (or plutocrats) who had unleashed the war.' " The positive attitude of the Soviet press toward Nazi Germany led some of the prisoners at Solovki to imagine a future alliance between the two countries: "They thought that Russia and Germany made the strongest combination in Europe and perhaps the world (not much notice of the United States was taken at that time), and believed that together they could break Great Britain once and for all."[16]

The Soviet historian Roy Medvedev notes that as a result of Molotov's speech "Beria gave a secret order to the GULAG administration forbidding camp guards to call political prisoners 'Fascists.' The order was rescinded only in June 1941."[17]

The Justification of Gaining Time

Both eyewitnesses and later Soviet publications explain and justify the Hitler-Stalin pact as a means by which the USSR "gained time" to prepare itself for the decisive battle against Nazi Germany. According to this view, the pact was a purely tactical maneuver, and the Soviet government continued to consider Fascism and Nazi Germany as the principal enemies. Viktor Kravchenko, who was a factory director in Kemerovo and knew many high Soviet officials, countered this theory in his memoirs:

> The theory that Stalin was merely "playing for time" while feverishly arming against the Nazis was invented much later, to cover up the Kremlin's tragic blunder in trusting Germany. It was such a transparent invention that little was said about it inside Russia during the Russo-German war; only after I emerged into the free world did I hear it seriously advanced and believed. It was a theory that ignored the most significant aspect of the Hitler-Stalin arrangement: the large-scale economic undertakings which drained the U.S.S.R. of the very products and materials and productive capacity necessary for its own defense preparations.[18]

Kravchenko's analysis is confirmed by my own experience. During the entire period of the Hitler-Stalin pact, from August 1939 to June 22, 1941, I never saw the slightest hint of such a view in Soviet publications. Even at meetings, where, on occasion, more was said than could be found in the press, there was never even a suggestion that the impact was concluded in order to gather our forces and prepare for an impending attack by Nazi Germany.

The argument of "gaining time" was first used after the German invasion of the Soviet Union on June 22, 1941. In his address delivered on July 3, 1941, Stalin had to defend the pact before the nation. "What did we gain by concluding the non-aggression pact with Germany?" Stalin asked in his favorite rhetorical fashion. As always, he provided the answer himself: "We secured our country peace for a year and a half, and the opportunity of preparing its forces to repulse Fascist Germany should she risk an attack on our country despite the pact."[19]

After this, the theory of "gaining time" acquired currency and had since become the obligatory explanation in the USSR. However, as Roy Medvedev remarked, "Soviet-German 'friend-ship' did delay the USSR's entry into the war by two years. But the delay was used more effectively by Germany than by the USSR. Seizing one country after another, Germany increased its military potential in those years much faster than the Soviet Union."[20]

Alexander Weissberg
in the "Inner Prison" in Kiev

At the time of the Hitler-Stalin pact, millions of men and women were in Soviet prisons and labor camps. The memoirs of three of these people, who later emigrated to the West, are discussed below. All three people were imprisoned in different parts of the Soviet Union, but all had one thing in common: none of them knew in August 1939 that the Soviet Union had concluded a pact with Nazi Germany. All three only learned of the pact weeks or months later, a fact which, in one way or another, had tragic effects on each of them.

Alexander Weissberg, an Austrian Communist and physicist, learned of the Hitler-Stalin pact in the "inner prison" in Kiev. Weissberg was born in Warsaw in 1901 to a wealthy businessman and his wife. He grew up in Vienna, studied physics, and in

1927 joined the Communist party of Austria. In 1931, Weissberg received a position in the Physical-Technical Institute in Kharkov, which was then one of the largest and best equipped research institutes in Europe. He worked with Leipunskij, who directed the department of nuclear fission, and with the famous Soviet physicist Landau.

At the end of 1937, Weissberg was arrested and accused of belonging to a terrorist group that intended to murder Stalin and Voroshilov while hunting in the Caucasus and to blow up the most important factories in Kiev upon the outbreak of war. During his years in prison, Weissberg experienced all the phases of captivity: solitary, discipline, and mass confinement. At first he was subjected to what is known in Soviet prisons as the "big conveyor"—an interrogation by three NKVD men in rotation for seven days and seven nights, with only two short breaks a day. Weissberg collapsed and signed a "confession," which he retracted twenty-four hours later. He was returned to the conveyor and collapsed again after four days and nights without sleep. He signed a new confession, retracted it later, and was again sent to the conveyor. It would have continued if not for two circumstances: Weissberg's Austrian passport assured him of a minimum of attention, and, more important, Albert Einstein and several Nobel prize winners in France intervened on his behalf. Einstein wrote a letter to Stalin on May 16, 1938. Thereafter, Weissberg's mistreatment diminished somewhat. He was transferred to the "inner prison" in Kiev, which had relatively clean cells and was not overcrowded, in contrast to the other prisons in which masses of people were detained. However, the total isolation was very painful. Nothing was said in a normal tone of voice; the guards whispered, even the prisoners had to whisper. The idleness was also burdensome. Weissberg had no pencil and paper, not a single book, and no contact with anyone whatsoever.

It was here that Weissberg learned of the Hitler-Stalin pact from a new prisoner, an official from Chernigov, north of Kiev. He had already been in prison there for one and a half years, but brought news from the newspapers: "We've made a pact of friendship with the Germans," he reported. "Ribbentrop himself was in Moscow, with Stalin, Molotov and all the rest of them. I wonder if Kaganovitch was there too. It would have been funny to see the Nazi and the Jew drinking to each other's health." Neither Weissberg nor the other inmates could grasp the meaning of this. None of them imagined that the pact meant the start of World War II.

After this, the prisoners received no more news; they didn't know that Germany invaded Poland on September 1, that the Second World War began several days later, and that Soviet troops crossed the Polish border on September 17 and later annexed the Eastern part of Poland. Only at the beginning of November 1939 did a new prisoner bring news from the outside world. He was a Bashkir from Ufa—large, big-boned, and slightly bent forward—who spoke Russian poorly. He had been the People's Commissar of the Workers and Peasants Control Organization of the Bashkirian Autonomous Republic. While traveling from Ufa to Moscow, he happened to get hold of a newspaper. "He told us that war had been declared, Germany against France and England and other confused statements. We didn't believe a word, since his information about a concerted action by the Soviet Union and Nazi Germany seemed so improbable."

Only three days later, the Bashkir's statements were confirmed by yet another new prisoner, a Soviet diplomat from Chung King, the provisional capital of China during the Japanese occupation. On Molotov's orders the diplomat had been requested by telegraph to return to Moscow, where he was arrested as soon as the airplane landed. This diplomat provided them for the first time with details of the development which had led to war. Alexander Weissberg found new hope: "Now that the block would be shattered and freedom would return and I should be able to go home. I assumed that my socialist friends had streamed into the armies of the Western European powers to fight against Hitler, and after a short rest in which to recuperate I proposed to join them."

But fate was against him. Only a few days later, Weissberg was transferred from the inner prison in Kiev to the Butyrka prison in Moscow. The "extradition cell" in the Butyrka "was a strange place," he recalls. "Let us suppose there was a house in No Man's Land, and that despite all the fighting the inhabitants still live on in it, but without going outside. Perhaps that gives some idea of the atmosphere which prevailed in our cell." Here Weissberg met other German emigrants, including Zenzl Mühsam, the widow of Erich Mühsam, the actress Carola Naher, and Margarete Buber-Neumann.

On December 31, 1939, Weissberg and several other prisoners were awakened early, brought to an almost luxurious bath, shaved, and taken to the dressing room where they were given excellent clothes. That afternoon Weissberg was called to a young NKVD officer who gave him a sheet of paper: "Read that and sign it, Citizen, please." The document explained that the proceedings against Alexander Weissberg had been adjourned *sine die* and that he was to be expelled "from the territory of the Union of Soviet Socialist Republics as an undesirable alien." But where was he being sent? "You will be sent to Germany" the First Lieutenant replied. "But I don't want to go to Germany," Weissberg countered. "I have nothing to do with Germany and I want nothing to do with German Fascism. I formally ask for permission to go to Sweden." However, nothing helped. The instructions were clear: Germany.

On New Year's Eve, 1939, Weissberg's train departed from Moscow.

Fifty physically and spiritually bruised and battered souls started on their return journey, from a country which they had freely chose to serve but which had rejected them, to a country which was their homeland but which had become foreign to them. They stood between the fronts. They had become home-less and rootless, in both countries. We traveled out of the Soviet Union into devastated Poland toward Brest-Litovsk. On the other side of the bridge over the Bug the representatives of another totalitarian system awaited us—the Gestapo.[21]

Evgenia Ginzburg:
The Pact in the Kolyma Labor Camp

The Hitler-Stalin pact influenced the lives of the prisoners in the Soviet Union in completely different ways. Alexander Weiss-berg was handed over to the Gestapo. Evgenia Ginzburg recalls in her memoirs that one of the prisoners with her was shot for a critical remark about the pact.

Until 1937, Evgenia Ginzburg was a convinced member of the Communist party in Kazan, the capital of the Tatar Auton-omous Soviet Republic. Her husband was a member of the Tatar Regional Committee of the party and she was a teacher and journalist for the party newspaper, *Krasnaya Tatariya.*

On February 7, 1939, she was called to the office of the Regional Committee of the party and, after several questions, was told to leave her party card there. With that, she was excluded from the party. Eight days later she was arrested and, during the first interrogation, accused of "belonging to the terrorist underground organization in the editorial board of *Kras-naya Tatariya*." Of course, no such organization had ever existed.

Evgenia Ginzburg was first sent to the NKVD prison in Kazan, where she was repeatedly interrogated and tortured. Later she was transferred to the Lefortovo prison in Moscow, then to the Lyubyanka, and finally to the Butyrka prison. There she met the German emigré actress Carola Neher, with whom she soon became friends. Finally, Ginzburg was placed in a cell which was intended almost exclusively for foreign Communists. Among these were Gerda Kästner and Klara, a German Communist who had first been tortured by the Gestapo and later by the NKVD; years later she still had frightful scars on her hips and behind. In this cell, which Ginzburg called the "Communist International," there was also a Latvian and a Chinese Communist; the latter had been a student at the Sun Yat Sen University in Moscow and later arrested.

Ginzburg was transferred from Moscow to Jaroslavl', where her original sentence of ten years of solitary confinement was commuted to ten years of forced labor. She was transferred together with other prisoners to a transit camp in Vladivostok in the Soviet Far East. The journey lasted more than a month under unspeakable conditions. They finally arrived in June of 1939. In August 1939, they were taken in an old ship, the Dzhurma, to the Bay of Nagaevo and then to the Magadan labor camp.

Ginzburg learned of the Hitler-Stalin pact on a winter day at the end of 1939:

It was the winter of 1939–1940. One of us got hold of a fairly recent number of *Pravda*, which caused a sensation when we read it that evening before "lights out." It contained the full text, with respectful comment, of Hitler's latest speech, and a two-page photograph of Molotov receiving von Ribbentrop. "A charming family group," remarked Katya Rotmistrovskaya as she climbed onto the upper bunk. This was careless of her: she had been warned often enough that people had been put among us who listened closely to what was said in the hut at night. Sure enough, six months later Katya was shot for "anti-Soviet agitation."[22]

Margarete Buber-Neumann: From Karaganda to Brest-Litovsk

Margarete Buber-Neumann was born in 1901, the daughter of an entrepreneur in Potsdam. She studied in Heidelberg and Jena, where she belonged to a socialist youth group. In 1926, she joined the Communist party of Germany. Soon she was working full-time for the Comintern journal *International Press Correspondence* (Inprecor), whose offices were in the Communist party headquarters in Berlin, the Karl Liebknecht Haus. From 1921 until 1932, she was, as she wrote, "a loyal member of the Communist party of Germany." She visited the Soviet Union several times, and her husband, Heinz Neumann, was twice invited by Stalin to Moscow. After Heinz Neumann was demoted from his position as the second most important official of the CP Germany in the spring of 1932, she accompanied him to Spain and later to Switzerland, which they left for Moscow in May of 1935.

Heinz Neumann was arrested during the night of April 27, 1937. Margarete, although still free, lost all that she had. Though nearly destitute, she went regularly to pay the cashier of the Lubyanka to improve her husband's living conditions. Finally, in July of 1938, she too was arrested and charged with being a "dangerous element to society." At first, she was placed in the Butyrka prison in Moscow and then condemned to a "corrective labor camp." Finally, after a long journey in a boxcar for prisoners, Margarete, No. 174475, reached the Karaganda camp in northern Kazakhstan.

Soon after her arrival the prisoners were distributed to different parts of the huge camp. Margarete and about eighty other men and women were sent to an area called Burma, a desolate, flat wasteland where no trees or bushes grew.

She only learned of the Hitler-Stalin pact long after August 23, 1939. She met the German Communist Grete Sonntag behind the latrine of the camp administration. They talked in whispers: " 'Do you think we'll ever get out of here now that Stalin's got this pact of friendship with Hitler?' she asked. 'We Communists are a bigger nuisance to him than ever now.' Her eyes filled with tears."

Only a few weeks later an event occurred that at first surprised Margarete Buber-Neumann and filled her with hope. Together with other German Communist prisoners such as Carola Neher, Betty Olberg, and Wally Adler, she was sent, under much improved conditions, back to the Butyrka prison in Moscow. There a soldier led them into a special room.

In the room two G.P.U. officers were sitting at a table, and they invited me in a friendly tone to take a seat. I did so. "How is your health? Do you feel quite well? Have you made a good recovery?". . . Their attitude was comforting. They ran through the papers on the desk before them.

"Have you relatives abroad?" one asked.

"Yes," I replied eagerly. This was it, then. "I have a sister in Paris and I have permission to go to France from the French Consulate. . . ."

He interrupted me: "No; I mean in Germany."

That was a shock. "What is to happen to me?" I blurted out. "Where are you going to send me?"

"I am not allowed to give you any information about that," he replied. "You will learn in due time. That's all."

Just as with Alexander Weissberg, the women were taken to the hairdresser's and then to a room full of lingerie, dresses, shoes, and fur coats, where they were asked in a friendly way what items of clothing they needed. A few days later they were brought to a room in the Butyrka where several NKVD officers were standing at a long table. Buber-Neumann was handed a paper:

It was a printed form, but in one place had been typed: "The sentence of five years' reformatory labour passed on Margarete Genrichovna Buber-Neumann is commuted into immediate expulsion from the territory of the Soviet Union."
"Sign it," he said and handed me a pen.

Shortly thereafter, she was taken to the "black raven," the prison transporter, which was already packed tightly with other German anti-Fascists. The vehicle stopped at a Moscow train station from which all the trains departed toward the West. The compartments had no windows—one could only get a peek at the outer world through the bars over the aisle.

During the entire journey, the prisoners—twenty-eight men and two women—were treated as never before. They were given cheese, bread, butter, tins of food, tea, and a pack of cigarettes every day. Those in charge of them were friendly but said nothing about their destination. They still hoped that they might be sent to Lithuania, which was still independent. However, on the morning of February 7, 1940, "we passed through Minsk and the train continued on its way to Poland. . . . Although I had thought we were to be sent back to Germany, I now realized how strongly I had clung to the faint hope that after all we should branch off at Minsk."

Later on the call rang out "Get ready with your things!" The bars were opened and the prisoners climbed down onto the train tracks and stood in the freezing winter air. In the distance they could recognize a train station: Brest-Litovsk.

> Betty and I, an old professor and a prisoner with a wounded leg were taken in on a lorry. The men had to walk. We got out on the Russian side of the Brest-Litovsk bridge and waited for them to come up, looking across the bridge into occupied Poland. The men arrived and then a group of G.P.U. men crossed the bridge. We saw them returning after a while, and the group was larger. There were S.S. officers with them. The S.S. commandant and the G.P.U. chief saluted each other. The Russian was a good head taller than the German. He took some papers from a bright leather case and began to read out a list of names. The only one I heard was "Margarete Genrichovna Buber-Neumann."[23]

Once on the German side, the prisoners were brought to a wooden shack; there they saw for the first time an SS cap with the skull and crossbones close up. They were taken in a boxcar to a prison in Bialas, a provincial Polish town in the German zone, then to Lublin, and finally to the Ravensbrück concentration camp where Margarete Buber-Neumann spent the next five years until the end of the war.

3

SHOCK WAVES IN THE WORLD
COMMUNIST MOVEMENT

The official Soviet history of the Communist International, published by the Institute of Marxism-Leninism of the Central Committee of the CPSU and translated into all the languages of the
"socialist" countries, deals only briefly with the impact of the
Hitler-Stalin pact on the world Communist movement. In fact,
in a book of more than 700 pages one finds only the following
reference: "Not everyone understood immediately the grounds
and motives for this act of the Soviet government in the realm
of foreign policy. The pact caused a certain lack of understanding
even among the ranks of other communist parties."[1]

A review of the newspapers in a number of countries, however,
proves that the impact of the pact was deeper, more serious,
and much more varied than the phrase "a certain lack of understanding" suggests. The newspapers describe the avalanches
of political change that the pact caused. Next, there are documents dealing with the illegal Communist movement in Germany, written in prisons, concentration camps, and by emigrés.
Last, we shall consider the memoirs of French Communists,
whose party was the strongest outside the Soviet Union, and of

other Communists from England, Italy, Hungary, Czechoslovakia, Yugoslavia, Belgium, Sweden, Switzerland, and the United States.

GERMAN COMMUNISTS UNDERGROUND: IN PRISONS, CONCENTRATION CAMPS, AND AS EMIGRES

The Mood of the Communists in the German Underground

The Hitler-Stalin pact was especially painful for the German Communists, whose opposition to Fascism in the underground was conducted under extremely harsh conditions. The following are three typical memoirs of Communists in Solingen, Stuttgart, and Hochheim, which bear witness to the conditions at the time.

Willi Dickhut, born in 1904, was a worker in Solingen and became an active member of the Communist party in 1926. He was arrested in 1933, but at the time of the pact was freed from prison and was working in the Communist underground. Dickhut left the following record of the impression that the pact made on the Communists in Solingen:

In August of 1939 the Soviet Union concluded a non-aggression pact with Nazi Germany which caused a tremendous sensation among the populace and utter bewilderment among the working class. Our illegal organization was now confronted by a very difficult situation. How could we explain the pact to the comrades, to our sympathizers and to class-conscious workers? We received no information or directives from above, but were assaulted with questions. Our contact with the regional Party leadership was broken since the comrade who had maintained contact with us was assigned other duties and not provided a successor. In short we were left to our own devices.

The Communists underground attempted to explain that the Soviet Union had to prevent a unified front among the capitalists; one capitalist country should be played off against another in order to strengthen the USSR. In any event, the Soviet Union needed to gain time in order to prepare itself militarily for the inevitable confrontation with German imperialism. "We will base our agitation on these principles in order to counteract the bewilderment."

According to Dickhut, no one today could imagine what this "bewilderment in our ranks" meant in this extremely difficult situation.[2] Denunciations were more common than ever before, and even reasonable people were infected by Nazi propaganda.

The Communists in the underground in Stuttgart were in a similar position. Eugen Eberle grew up in a working-class family and joined the Communist party of Germany in 1928. In addition to his political activity, he was interested in literature, history, and Marxist theory. He taught at the Marxist Workers' School (MASCH) for several years. In March 1933, he too was arrested and sent to the Heuberg prison camp. After his release he was again active in the anti-Fascist resistance. He recalled that "my Communist friends and I were speechless when the Soviet Union and the Nazi government, that is the German Reich, concluded a non-aggression pact and a friendship treaty in the Summer of 1939. On August 23, 1939, Minister of Foreign Affairs von Ribbentrop and Molotov signed these agreements in Moscow on the instructions of Hitler and Stalin respectively. We had absolutely no idea how the Soviet Union could conclude such agreements with Nazi Germany." To be sure, Eberle and others heard foreign radio broadcasts about "purges" in the Soviet Union, but they still felt the greatest aversion toward the Hitler-Stalin pact.

However, they overcame their first bout of political consternation. "Trustful as we were we considered the German-Soviet agreement a legitimate albeit temporary means of defending the USSR."[3]

The Communists in Hochheim, near Erfurt in Thuringia, felt similar qualms. Paul Elflein came from a working-class family and joined the Communist party in 1920. In 1923, he was appointed Chairman of the Hochheim Communist organization. Despite all of his party work, he still became, by the end of the 1920s, critical of the "dependency of the CP Germany on Moscow" and concerned that the Communist movement would become "more and more an instrument of Russian foreign policy." In June of 1929, he read in a Communist newspaper that he had been excluded from the CP Germany. He joined the KPO (Communist Party Opposition) led by Brandler and Thalheimer. Elflein was especially close to Alfred Schmidt, who had long been an active party official, a Communist delegate in the Prussian state parliament, and a member of the CPO. Elflein wrote:

1939—the news of a non-aggression pact between the Soviet Union and Nazi Germany. I immediately ran for a newspaper in order to convince myself that it was true. Indeed, there were the telegrams, published. I wouldn't have believed it possible. Despite all the criticism, Stalin was still the hope of all anti-Fascists. And now, an agreement with Hitler. With the exception of Alfred Schmidt no one whom I asked approved of the pact.[4]

Erich Honecker and Heinz Brandt:
Two Observers in the Brandenburg Prison

Erich Honecker, who was himself a prisoner, recalled that there were some 3,000 inmates in the Brandenburg prison in 1939, of which about 2,200 were political prisoners. Two of these recorded their very different eyewitness impressions of how the Communist prisoners reacted to the Hitler-Stalin pact.

Erich Honecker's recollection of the event is relatively positive. Honecker, who was twenty-seven years old at the time of the pact, was born in Wiebelskirchen in the Saarland. He joined the CP Germany in 1929. From August 1930 until August 1931, he attended the Lenin School in Moscow, the main training center for foreign Communists. After he returned to Germany from Moscow, he was appointed director of the German Communist Youth Federation (KJVD) in the Saarland. When Hitler seized power in 1933, Honecker was given the task of expanding the Communists' underground organization in Mannheim, Frankfurt/Main, and the surrounding region.

On December 4, 1935, Honecker was arrested in Berlin and sent to the Gestapo headquarters on Prince Albrecht Street. In June 1937, he was sentenced by the senate of the People's Court to ten years in prison. In July of the same year, he was transferred to the prison in Brandenburg-Görden.

According to Honecker, the news of the Hitler-Stalin pact engendered very little discussion:

When in the early morning of 24 August 1939 Nazi newspapers reported the signing of the treaty, Max Uecker and myself organized a get-together with Max Maddalena and Fritz Groisse in the dentist's waiting cell before 7 A.M. We were agreed that the signing of the treaty was a diplomatic success for the Soviet Union which thus escaped the danger of having to face a unified bloc of the imperialist powers. At the same time it retained its freedom of action and gained time to strengthen its defence potential. Further developments were to confirm our joint thinking which was shared by most political prisoners.[5]

A more thorough and probably truer description of the event is found in the memoirs of another inmate of the Brandenburg prison, Heinz Brandt. Brandt, who was thirty years old at the time, grew up in Berlin; he joined the KJVD in 1928 and the CP Germany in 1931. However, from the beginning he was critical of the official party line, which was almost totally concerned with fighting the "social Fascism" of the Socialist party of Germany. Brandt, who had been active in the Communist election campaign in Berlin-Weißensee, was arrested on March 5, 1933, shortly after Hitler took power. Held prisoner and beaten in the basement of a building belonging to the SA, he was then set free and immediately resumed his illegal activity. He was arrested a second time and given a long prison term for having distributed an illegal Communist newspaper (the *Siemens Loudspeaker*) among workers and for "preparing high treason." In the prison of Brandenburg-Görden he witnessed a polarization of political views and the formation of two groups of Communist prisoners:

A different breeze blew among the political prisoners in the Brandenburg prison than in Luckau. More and more prisoners came who were full-time officials of the Communist Party. The split between two groups became clearer: Those who were true to the Party line, who had never forgotten and never learnt anything, were hardened even more by prison and had blind faith in the policy of Stalin and the Comintern. They slander the slightest doubt as the onset of "decay." Those who were true to the Party found support in the arrest of entire groups of top Party officials.

However the second group, composed of reflective Communists, is also growing. This group includes all those comrades of the SPD, SAP, KPO, Trotskyites and the New Beginning group, who had ceased to be Stalinists long ago. We attempt to exchange our views among each other and to make them comprehensible to die-hards. However the more problematic the Comintern's policy seemed in the light of events, the more heatedly the die-hards debated.

The most important points were, according to Heinz Brandt, the Moscow "show trials," the Spanish Civil War, and the Hitler-Stalin pact. Before the Hitler-Stalin pact there had, according to Brandt, always been a sense of solidarity among the political prisoners:

> Despite all of our internal differences we stuck together in the face of the prison administration. That was the implicit precondition even during the most bitter discussions. The system of mutual moral, intellectual and material help—the exchange of ideas, information, notes, newspapers, food, tobacco—was well developed and functioned marvellously. We were a big family, and disputes were family quarrels.

Brandt explained that the political prisoners were on good terms with some of the wardens as well as with the prisoners who worked in the electrical repair shop, both of whom were used to listening to foreign news broadcasts.

However, by the time of the Hitler-Stalin pact there was no longer one big family. Brandt recalled that

> with the non-aggression pact between Hitler and Stalin the situation became dangerous. Those who were absolutely loyal to the Party line greeted the conclusion of the so-called non-aggression pact in August 1939 because it unleashed the desired war between the "imperialists." The rest of us, how-

ever, were extremely dismayed by this evil betrayal of the international working class which revealed to the world that Stalin's state, although outwardly different from Hitler's, was also an inhuman despotism. We used to write "it takes one to know one" and "birds of a feather flock together" to our relatives in a harmless, personal context so that our letters would pass the prison censors.

However, there was a group between those who advocated and those who opposed the pact: "Between them were some who preferred to listen than to speak their minds. They didn't want to commit themselves, since the Stalinists constantly threatened them by saying 'Some day the Party will call you to account for your deviations and your criticism which is hostile to the Party.' "

The debate about the pact poisoned the relations between the prisoners and was carried over into more and more topics.

When confronted with such embittered discussions the Stalinists burst the bonds of solidarity. The situation became very difficult. The majority of the Party people who had been undecided and still full of illusions was downcast, in despair and vascillated between us and the die-hards. Some said that they didn't understand in the least why everything was happening. They didn't agree with the arguments of the die-hards but said that one had to trust Stalin and the Soviet Union. There would certainly be some sound although mysterious and as yet unknown reasons for the pact. . . . A good number of political prisoners began to approve of the pact in the illusory hope that it would lead to a general amnesty of anti-Fascists and freedom for us and Ernst Thälmann. That was the least which Stalin would demand from Hitler.

However, the critical Communists, of which Heinz Brandt was one, considered this wishful thinking: "We knew that not amnesty but war was around the corner." These critical Communists began to systematically formulate their views of the pact. They had five theses:

1. "Fascism, especially Nazism, is a mortal danger for human society. Whosoever concludes a pact with fascists commits a crime."

2. "The conclusion of this pact in the name of the supposed interests of the supposed working class is not an error but a betrayal of Socialism, of the great idea of the friendship among peoples, of international fraternity, just like the 4th of August, 1914" (when the Social Democrats in the German Reichstag voted for war credits).

3. "The non-aggression pact provides historical proof that Stalinism is not a dictatorship of the proletariat but a dictatorship over the proletariat."

4. "The III International (Comintern) has shown itself to be a mere appendage of Stalinist foreign policy, an instrument of the Stalinist system of terror. The Comintern will display itself in the Second World War as a 'putrifying body' as did the Second International in the First World War."

5. "The present catastrophe proves that the international workers' movement must break with the terrorist despotism and begin anew by rebuilding on a completely new and democratic foundation. Our struggle against Fascism can only be morally and politically legitimized by a humanistic, socialist and democratic platform. Fascism can only be overthrown and overcome with such a fundamental concept."

Heinz Brandt concluded that

the Hitler-Stalin Pact was not the expression of a temporary and limited common interest but of a partial conformity between Fascism and Stalinism despite their different social, historical and intellectual roots and social orders. . . . Whosoever saw, as we did, Fascism as a mortal enemy could not neglect its accomplice Stalinism and was obliged also to oppose the latter.[6]

Eugen Ochs: Biblical Scholars and Communists in Dachau

Inmates in other prisons and concentration camps also had serious discussions about the pact, although these may not have been so clearly formulated as in the Brandenburg prison. Eugen Ochs recalled the discussions in the concentration camp in Dachau. Ochs, a trained mechanic, joined the CP Germany in 1925 and was an active party official and member of the workers' council from the late 1920s. Like Paul Elflein who was mentioned earlier, Ochs was a member of the KPO, which supported a unified trade union movement and which disapproved of using the term "Social Fascism" to oppose the Social Democrats. After Hitler's seizure of power, Ochs joined the anti-Fascist resistance in Stuttgart, was arrested in December of 1934, and was soon transferred to the concentration camp in Dachau near Munich. There, as prisoner No. 32600, he frequently met the Social Democrat Kurt Schumacher, who was also an inmate.

Ochs was less surprised by the Hitler-Stalin pact than the Communists quoted above. Ochs was imprisoned at the time with other convicts who were Biblical scholars who had been arrested because they would not take the oath to Hitler and refused to serve in the army. The Biblical scholars formed a labor gang which was sent every Monday morning by truck to Sudelfeld near Bayrischzell, where they had to work on construction sites for the SS. They returned to the camp every Saturday. Since the construction projects lasted for weeks, the scholars got to know their guards. One day they reported that the SS men had told them that the Germans and Russians had agreed to the partition of Poland.

Ochs and the other prisoners couldn't believe this. They thought that the Biblical scholars understood too little about politics and had allowed the SS men to pull their legs. A few weeks later, however, they realized that the Biblical scholars had been right. Ochs recalled:

> In August, 1939 the story told by the Biblical scholars to the effect that the Germans and Russians had agreed to the partition of Poland, was confirmed. Poland's fate was sealed by the non-aggression pact between Nazi Germany and the Soviet Union. The political prisoners found this event incomprehensible: We simply could not understand how Fascists and communists could agree to anything.[7]

Wolfgang Abendroth: Discussion in the Luckau Prison

Wolfgang Abendroth (1906–1985), born in Elberfeld, joined the socialist youth movement but soon switched to the KJVD. While in law school he was a member of the Communist student organization (*Kostufra*). At the end of the 1920s, he switched to the KPO and for a time was also a member of the "New Beginning" movement.

After Hitler seized power at the beginning of 1933, Abendroth joined the resistance and was arrested in Berlin on February 22, 1937. He was first sent to the Gestapo prison on

Prince Albrecht Street and in November of the same year was transferred to the Luckau prison in Niederlausitz. There the cells were overfilled: four prisoners were in each one-man cell. About two-thirds of the prisoners were political, one-third criminals. The prison administration intentionally placed at least one criminal in each cell in order to watch over the political prisoners. According to Wolfgang Abendroth, the criminals were so unsuspecting that the political prisoners could easily deceive them.

The political prisoners numbered, according to Abendroth, approximately 1,000. Of these, only two or three were members of the KPO, several of the International Socialist Combat League (ISK) and the Socialist Workers' Party (SAP), and about ten of various social democratic groups; all the rest were members of the CP Germany. There were many discussions among the political prisoners about the "political line," especially with the members of the CP Germany. Among the latter were some who were not unswervingly loyal to the party. Discussions were held in a spirit of comraderie—even with the "most die-hard CP members." The prisoners had discussed the Moscow show trials, and some CP members had declared that they couldn't believe the accusations of the prosecution. During the last week of August 1939, the prisoners learned of the Hitler-Stalin pact:

> After the conclusion of the non-aggression pact between Hitler and Stalin I provoked a heated debate, a bitter factional struggle, by decisively taking a position against the treaty. . . . I characterized the pact as the 4th of August, 1914 for the Communist International. . . . At the beginning of the debate the proponents of the pact outnumbered the opponents by about 2:1. . . . This showed that the old dividing line between the factions was blurred. The question was discussed very polemically by both sides.[8]

Curiously, in his memoirs published in 1976, Abendroth modified his categoric rejection of the pact, stating that, in the light of later experience, the Soviet Union was compelled to conclude such an agreement. To the best of my knowledge, this is the only case in which an opponent of the pact changed his mind thirty years later and began to excuse and justify the treaty. As a rule, the opposite occurred; many of those who considered the pact necessary at the time and who supported it with some reservations, later recognized that its true purpose was the territorial expansion of Germany and the USSR at the expense of smaller nations, and criticized or rejected it.

The Leaders of the CP Germany in Paris

Not only many of the rank and file members of the German Communist party but even party leaders who had emigrated to Paris were surprised by the pact. The head of the party leadership, which was known as the Central Committee of the CP Germany, was Franz Dahlem (1892–1981), who had been a member since 1920. At first, he was primarily active in the Rhineland; in 1928, he was appointed to the Central Committee of the party and was a Communist delegate in the German Reichstag. He was also the party's intermediary with the press attaché of the Soviet embassy in Berlin.

After working for the CP Germany for a short time in Berlin, Dahlem emigrated to Prague and Paris. During the Spanish Civil War, he was the political director of the international brigades. After the defeat of the Spanish Republic, he returned to Paris in the spring of 1939.

Dahlem's memoirs, which were published in East Germany, reveal that none of the leaders of the German CP in Paris foresaw the Hitler-Stalin pact. Up until the second half of Au-

gust 1939, the German CP leadership "had considerable freedom for legal, independent, political and cultural activity. For
example, up until the last week of August we published regularly, legally and without hindrance our political magazine
the *Deutsche Volkszeitung*. . . . As far as I can remember the
French censors did not interfere seriously during the entire
time."

The last issue of the *Deutsche Volkszeitung*, dated August
27, 1939, appeared on August 24. It published a long cal-
endar of events of various "friendship groups" that organized
lectures and discussions. On August 31 at 8:30 P.M., for
example, there was to be a "serious and gay evening of dialects" with "samples of various German dialects." However, this meeting never took place: "Already on the night
of August 23 and on the following nights the Paris police
arrested the first Communists in their apartments or hotels
and took them to the 'Sante,' " recalled Franz Dahlem. The
Sante was the infamous prison for those considered a danger
to state security. At first, however, only a small group of
German Communist emigrés was involved. Dahlem recalled
that "we were unprepared for the sudden blows of the class
enemy."

The change brought about by the Hitler-Stalin pact and
the fear of many Frenchmen of a German attack loosened
the bonds between the populace and the political emigrés.
According to Franz Dahlem, the French increasingly used
the contemptuous term *boche*, an abusive name for Germans
from the First World War. Increasing numbers of French
wanted to have nothing to do with the *boches*. "The worst
taint, however, which an emigré could have at that time was
to be suspected of being a Communist. . . . The eight days
before the beginning of the war was a complicated, even

critical period" for the Secretariat of the Central Committee
of the CP Germany.[9]

Alexander Abusch and the Official
Statement of the CP Germany

Of course the Central Committee of the CP Germany had to
issue an appropriate official statement on the pact. This task
was given to the emigré party officials Gerhart Eisler and Anton
Ackermann, together with Alexander Abusch (1902–1982). Alexander Abusch was born in Cracow and raised in Nürnburg.
He belonged to the CP Germany from its founding at the end
of 1918 and took an active part in the uprisings in Bavaria and
Thuringia. In 1924, he became editor-in-chief of the Communist
newspaper *Neue Zeitung* in Jena, then a member of the CP
Germany's press service and an editor of the *Rote Fahne*; from
1928 to 1933, he was editor-in-chief of the Communist newspaper *Ruhrecho*, published in Essen. In 1933, Abusch moved
to the Saar region, which was not controlled by Germany and
where he was editor-in-chief of the *Arbeiterzeitung*. He traveled
to Prague and then to Paris, where, as an active party official,
he was unquestioningly loyal to the party line. In his memoirs,
published in East Germany, he recalled:

> Of course we ruminated about the reasons, perspectives
> and arguments. We were insulted as "Bolshevik bureaucrats"
> because, despite all the reflection on the new events, we were,
> from the very beginning, determined to be Rocks of Gibraltar
> in mastering this difficult situation. . . . In the Jardin du
> Luxembourg I met Franz Dahlem sitting on a park bench.
> From the first moment we were in complete agreement on the

non-agression pact: now more than ever we were to do everything for the Soviet Union![10]

Abusch, Eisler, and Ackermann prepared the draft of the
statement of the Central Committee of the CP Germany on
the German-Soviet nonaggression pact. The task was, as
Abusch recalled, not an easy one, since the CP Germany
was "in the position of waging an anti-imperialist war on
two fronts." It was important for the German Communists
to "grasp the dialectic of the flow of events and thereby the
position of the Soviet Union from a geopolitical and strategic
point of view."[11]

The resulting draft was accepted on August 25 by the emigré
Secretariat of the CP Germany with only minor changes; apparently, these party officials were left to their own devices
because neither Franz Dahlem nor Alexander Abusch mention
an instruction or directive from Moscow in their otherwise detailed memoirs. Had there been such instructions, they would
certainly have said so.

The statement of the CP Germany of August 25, 1939,
applauds the pact as an "act of the Soviet Union for peace."
People should support the conclusion of similar "peace
agreements" with Poland, France, England, Rumania, and
other countries. Hitler had concluded the agreement in a
desperate situation, and only the entire German people could
be the guarantors of its observation. For that, however, the
German people would have to "take the fate of the German
nation in its hands." The future of Germany depends first
and foremost on the working class. The goal was to form
a "revolutionary, unified party" to achieve the necessary
unity and to gather the German people into an "anti-Fascist
popular front."[12]

In fact, both the thrust and the formulation of the CP's

statement—drafted without instructions from Moscow—was at odds both with Moscow's policy and the reality of the anti-Fascist opposition in Germany.

Criticism Among the German Emigrés

The memoirs of Franz Dahlem and Alexander Abusch scarcely mention criticism among the German Communists. Only one brief episode in Abusch's memoirs hint at the resistance that loyal CP officials encountered among the rank and file. Alexander Abusch recorded a meeting with German writers who were also party members living in France: Gustav Regler and Alfred Kantorowicz, who had arrived "in utter despair" from the south of France. "The pact! The pact! How could Stalin do that to us?" was their first question. Abusch tried, as he emphasized in his memoirs, to patiently explain the actions of the Soviet Union. Kantorowicz slowly appeared to be open to his arguments in favor of the pact, but Regler continued to protest. Abusch commented that "our position as Communists became more precarious, since the allies of yesterday could become the enemies of today."[13]

Henry Jacoby, a former German Communist, was among the critical emigrés in France. During the Weimar Republic, he had been active in the Marxist youth and workers' movement. He was in the group of Marxist psychologists led by Manes Sperber, and, because of the growing threat of Fascism, he joined the CP Germany in 1930, although with certain reservations. He left the CP when the party leadership maintained that the German working class had not suffered a defeat as a result of Hitler's rise to power in 1933, and joined the illegal, left-socialist group known as *Der Funke* ("the Spark").

At the end of June 1934, Jacoby was arrested and condemned to two years and three months in prison. He was released from the Brandenburg prison at the end of June 1936 and emigrated to Prague and then to Paris, where he learned of the rapprochement between Germany and the USSR before the Hitler-Stalin pact was announced:

> Rumors spread about an alliance between Hitler and Stalin. The "Spark" group took these rumors seriously, especially after obtaining information from a Polish friend. The Communists and their adherents suspected nothing, and considered the possibility of an alliance as not worth discussing. They attributed the rumors to "Fascist-Trotskyite riff-raff." Their goal was to maintain the popular front against Hitler and for the defense of the Soviet Union; the newspaper *Deutsche Volkszeitung* even wanted this alliance to include the Pope. When the pact between Hitler and Stalin was announced it was declared to embody the "will of the people for peace."[14]

Jacoby had a group of critical socialist friends who attempted to apprehend the collapse of the political world in which they lived.

> The mighty workers' movement in Central Europe was in ruins; Hitler's tanks dominated Europe; Lenin's comrades-in-arms during the Russian Revolution had all been shot as spies; the Spanish Republic had been abandoned by the European democracies, its revolutionary movement stabbed in the back by Soviet agents and finally Stalin had concluded a pact with Hitler.
>
> It proved difficult to question that which had been learned and to tear one's self away from the ideas and thought processes of the past. Those who could not overcome the myth of the Russian Revolution had the most

difficulty. We were like flotsam and jetsam, cast ashore by the waves in this provincial town, the wreckage of a sunken ship, but we still couldn't believe that we had taken the wrong course.[15]

The "Bureaucracy Discussion" in Montauban

The provincial town to which Henry Jacoby referred was the French town of Montauban, where a group of German socialist and Marxist emigrés found refuge from the advancing German army. To their surprise, they found an excellent public library there and soon discovered hidden treasures. Jacoby and his friends became interested in documents from the period of the struggle between the monarchy and the aristocracy, and in particular, the growth of the bureaucracy and the development of its power.

The little group soon learned that the common Marxist view of the conflict between the aristocracy and the bourgeoisie failed to take into account some of the most important aspects of the rise of the nation state. With suspense, the scattered band of comrades read documents from the 17th Century, in which the nobles compared the reign of Louis XIV with an Oriental despotism and deplored the constant growth of the bureaucracy. But the bureaucracy continued to grow. Even the French Revolution did not eliminate it. In a yellowed notebook, Henry Jacoby found a quotation from St. Just: "The laws are revolutionary, those who implement them are not. The more the people is replaced by officials, the less democracy there is."

As a result of his research on the nature and role of the bureaucracy in the triumph of absolutism, Jacoby concluded that Soviet society should be characterized as one of bureaucratic rule. However, Jacoby's attempt to gain a better understanding of the present by examining the past met with some opposition within his group.

In particular, his thesis that Soviet society should be characterized as one of bureaucratic despotism was rejected at the beginning. The members of the Montauban study group all opposed Stalinism and were not adherents of Trotsky. However, they considered, as did Jacoby up until that time, Russia after the revolution to be a socialist workers' state— one that had been betrayed by Stalin and had strayed from the right path because of his regime. This situation ended because the group was still spellbound by the myth of the Rusian Revolution and collectivization of the means of production. Abandoned was Jacoby's denial that the fundamental character of the Soviet Union was socialist. Also abandoned was the fact that he was able to conceive of a social order neither capitalist nor socialist. This was too much for some to bear, not only because such a hypothetical order destroyed the hope that Russia would return to "true" socialism, but also because of the the faith that remained in the "iron laws of history," which dictated that capitalism would be replaced by socialism.

However, Jacoby reports that some of the members of the group embraced this interpretation in later years and discarded their "faith in Russia."[16]

J. K. in London:
A Cigar to Celebrate the Pact

The critical socialists from Montauban can be contrasted with Jürgen Kuczynski, who was then the leader of the emigré members of the CP Germany in London, England, and who was loyal to the party line.

Jürgen Kuczynski was born in Elberfeld in 1904, the son of a banker. He studied in Berlin, Heidelberg, and Erlangen, and joined the Communist party in 1930. He was soon the business editor of the party's newspaper *Rote Fahne*. After 1933, he emigrated to Prague, was in the Soviet Union for a short time, and, in October 1936, went to Paris, where he received instructions to go to England as the political leader of the German Communist emigrés. He fulfilled this function from October 1936 until 1941.

Kuczynski's Communist group had the task of writing leaflets and printing or copying them with the help of English comrades. They were then to distribute the leaflets to German sailors or try to have them smuggled into Germany. At the same time, they were supposed to discuss the situation in Nazi Germany in publications and lectures and thereby mobilize all possible forces among the German emigrés in England against Fascism. The Hitler-Stalin pact was concluded during the midst of this activity.

In his memoirs, published in East Germany, Jürgen Kuczynski always refers to himself in the third person, as J. K. J. K.'s reaction to the pact was unusual, especially when compared with the reactions of other eyewitnesses mentioned previously.

Of course the conclusion of the pact between the Soviet Union and Nazi Germany in August 1939 caused astonishment. J. K. discussed the situation immediately with leading comrades. Before he met them, however, he went to the best tobacconist in Belsize Park and bought a big cigar. All the comrades knew how much J. K. liked to smoke cigars and that, since cigars were extremely expensive in England, an emigre could only enjoy this pleasure if he received the cigar as a gift. While lighting his cigar J. K. explained to the comrades that it was "to celebrate the pact which can keep the Soviet Union out of a war." It was just a gesture, but even today a comrade occasionally reminds him of that meeting and of the feeling of certainty which the cigar gave them. [17]

Paris: Thorwald Siegel's Way Out

While Jürgen Kuczynski smoked a cigar in London to celebrate the pact, a German emigré in Paris, Thorwald Siegel, was so shaken and bewildered that he committed suicide.

Thorwald Siegel never wrote his own memoirs, but he is mentioned in the memoirs of Theodor Balk, a loyal Communist who came from Yugoslavia and was active in the CP Germany during the 1920s. Balk was arrested in Berlin in 1933 and fled from Germany after his release. He traveled illegally to Paris, where he met Thorwald Siegel, who offered to let him live in his apartment. Fortunately, Siegel got on well with the concierge of his apartment house. On the first evening, he introduced Balk to the concierge, explaining that Balk was his cousin who was visiting Paris for a short time.

After the conclusion of the Hitler-Stalin pact, there were endless discussions between the independent-minded Siegel and the die-hard Balk. Siegel immediately took the point of view that "the war could have been avoided if the Soviet Union had not concluded this pact." He repeated over and over again that "the country of socialism has allied itself with the Fascist Third Reich" and "started a war by concluding the Hitler-Stalin Pact."

One evening, as Siegel and Balk were on their way home, the former asked the latter to come to his apartment for a minute.

When they arrived, Siegel opened a suitcase and removed a package wrapped in paper. He removed the paper and placed a bottle with a wide neck on the table. It was cyanide, which Siegel had obtained from a laboratory in case he should be arrested by the Nazis.

Siegel compared the Hitler-Stalin pact to the betrayal by the Social Democratic leaders of their internationalist positions upon the outbreak of the First World War. He returned so frequently to the comparison between 1914 and 1939—the response of the Second International at the outbreak of the war in August 1914 and that of the Third International in August 1939—that he used only the shorthand "14" and "39." Siegel maintained that "then as now the workers' leaders have abandoned their ideals: in '14 the Second, in '39 the Third International. In '14 by shifting from opponents to supporters of war, today by concluding a pact with Hitler, the archenemy of the working class."

Theodor Balk retorted that one had to have confidence in their leaders and in the Communist International. Confidence? Thorwald Siegel was not impressed by this argument.

What did they say in '14 to the workers who watched in amazement as their leaders made an about-face? They said: "Trust your experienced leaders and not your eyes. Your leaders are not making an about-face, it only seems so." And so the workers trusted them, and that was a mistake, a fundamental mistake. And what do you say to me today? Have trust, even though your leaders appear to be making an about-face. Yes, if the Russians had only not erred so often. The show trials, the executions. He had been silent then because he did not trust that his judgement would be final. But now, now he saw clearly: A straight line led from the show trials to the pact. . . . Why did they tell the world that Tukhachevskij was a dangerous Nazi when they now walk arm-in-arm with Nazis?

Theodor Balk pointed to the treaty of Munich and the attempt of the Western powers to drive the Third Reich and the Soviet Union into a conflict with one another. The truth, he believed, was not to be found in photographs of Stalin and von Ribbentrop standing next to one another or in the signatures, united so suddenly and unexpectedly on an agreement. The goal, he believed, was simple: time, gain time so that the Soviet Union would be militarily prepared in the hour of truth. "Although we discussed the matter a hundred times, Thorwald Siegel was still not convinced." However, he saw that Siegel vacillated to a certain degree, which not only perplexed Balk but made him anxious: "The bottle of poison, which had disappeared from sight, now suddenly reappeared."

The following day was a Sunday. As usual, Theodor Balk was drinking his second cup of coffee with Thorwald Siegel at noon when they heard the voice of a boy in the street hawking newspapers, crying "Russians invade Poland!" And so they began their one hundred and first discussion:

"Voila!" said Thorwald Siegel. "Now there is no longer any point in discussing. Simply no point. They're all the same." I believe that an action does not have to have the same meaning when two different people do it. The Russians invaded Poland for strategic reasons, in preparation for the German invasion of the Soviet Union, which was sure to come.

Ach, Siegel knew these words from countless German explanations: With such words of concern for their own safety the Nazis broke all their treaties, remilitarized the Rhineland, occupied Prague, invaded Poland.

I grope for other arguments. These territories are inhabited by Ukrainians; according to the Curzon line they should have been transferred to the Soviet Union in 1920. In fact they were annexed by Poland. Isn't it better for the Ukrainians to be united with the rest of their people in a socialist republic than to live under the Nazi yoke?

Siegel had also heard this song all too often. Hitler had annexed Austria, occupied the Sudetenland and unleashed a war against Poland all under the pretext of the right of peoples for self-determination.

Balk tried one last time to change his friend's mind, saying, "Wait, Thorwald Siegel, just you wait!" But Siegel didn't change his mind. "Wait? There's no point in waiting any longer." The two parted; Theodor Balk spent this Sunday afternoon in Paris taking a long walk and only returned to the apartment in the evening. There he found Thorwald Siegel dead, having committed suicide.[18]

German Opposition in the Netherlands: "The News Created a Shock"

The term "shock" to describe the effect of the pact on the German emigrés and anti-Fascists is not only found in the memoirs of those who later broke with the party. Even Ewald Munschke, who was a Major General in the East German National People's Army when his memoirs were published, uses this term. Ewald Munschke was born in Berlin in 1901 and joined the Communist party in 1923. From the beginning of the 1930s he was in the party's military-political organization. After Hitler seized power, Munschke emigrated to the USSR, where he attended the Communist University for the Peoples of the West. During the Spanish Civil War, he was first the political commissar of a company in the XIIIth International Brigade. He took part in the battles in the Sierra Nevada Mountains and then on the front in Madrid.

After the fall of the Spanish Republic, Munschke was instructed to go to the Netherlands with a false passport, where he lived at the time of the Hitler-Stalin pact. "One should not conceal the fact that the news of the signing of the German-Soviet non-aggression pact created a shock among the emigres. Heated discussions took place," wrote Munschke, who himself remained true to the party line.

Because Munschke's memoirs were published by the military press in East Berlin, we must assume that he did not intend to be ironic when he wrote: "The thorough knowledge acquired during my years in the Soviet Union helped me to understand more quickly the reason underlying the tactical manoeuvres of Soviet policy. I avidly jumped into the debates being held: More than ever before it was important to discipline the comrades to iron unity."[19]

Heinz Kühn in Brussels: A Wedding or a Celebration of the Pact?

None of the memoirs of German Communists describe the reaction of the emigrés in Belgium; it is, however, described in the memoirs of the well-known Social Democrat Heinz Kühn, who was well informed about the Communists.

Heinz Kühn was born in a working-class family in Cologne. In 1928, he joined the socialist youth group known as the Falcons. He studied economics at the University of Cologne and in October 1931 joined the social democratic paramilitary organization known as the *Reichsbanner*. After Hitler seized power, Kühn was arrested and imprisoned in Cologne, only to continue his illegal activity upon his release. Later on, he was active in the Sudetenland in Czechoslovakia, smuggling socialist pamphlets into Germany by printing them on thin, crease-resistant paper and sewing them into the clothing lining of people who were crossing the border, or putting them in balloons and entrusting them to the wind. Kühn was sent to Belgium in June 1936, where he was to help with a social democratic newspaper entitled *Freies Deutschland.* He learned of the Hitler-Stalin pact in Brussels in an unusual manner:

> Hitler and Stalin concluded their pact on August 23, 1939; Marianne and I concluded ours on August 26: we wed. It had taken a long time for her to illegally obtain from Germany the papers which she needed to marry. And now we wanted, despite the imminent threat before us, to legalize our relationship with a simple civil ceremony. We celebrated our marriage that evening with our friends as young people do with a guitar, a harmonica and songs. It was the last happy evening for a long time: The next morning officers of the *Surete Publique* knocked at our door. We thought at first that they had come because of the noise which we had made, but no: "You celebrated the German-Soviet pact yesterday evening." Only when we showed them our marriage certificate and other papers was the angry denunciation of our neighbor drowned in laughter and wishes for happiness.

Apart from this very personal experience, Kühn describes the effect of the pact on the German Communist emigrés in Belgium:

> From our couriers we learned that the pact between the "red Vatican" and the brown devil was considered blasphemy by the remaining illegal cadres of the CP Germany. They not only lost their faith in the Party, there were also personal tragedies: How could they understand, for example, that over night the word "Fascist" disappeared from the vocabulary of every Communist official and that not Hitler but the Western powers bore the guilt of the war? Prepared for bitter discussions we looked for the Communist officials in their favorite pubs in Brussels, but couldn't find a single one.[20]

Karl Kunde: Confusion in the Cepoy Internment Camp

The discussion about the Hitler-Stalin pact ended by no means after a few days but continued for months, especially in French internment camps, in which many German anti-Fascists were interned. This we know from Karl Kunde, a metalworker who was born in Neustettin in 1904 and who joined the CP Germany in his youth. In 1933, he too began the journey through illegal activity, arrest, concentration camp, and emigration. On September 4, 1939, he was arrested as a foreigner in Paris; after many stops he finally arrived, at the beginning of April 1940, in the Cepoy internment camp in the Loire Departement. It was there that he and 500 other internees learned of the Hitler-Stalin pact. Kunde recalls the following: "The Hitler-Stalin pact also caused frightful confusion in our ranks. The pact was the subject of exhaustive discussions among us Communists." Then as now, Kunde defended the pact, but clearly saw how grave its consequences were: "These discussions demoralized many and reduced the number in our group. We were no longer united and that had practical consequences for our work in the camp. We now considered it our primary task simply to maintain the camp's Communist apparatus. Those who weren't fully behind us were excluded, but this increased our isolation. It was a difficult time."

Heinrich Brandler, who, together with August Thalheimer, directed the CP opposition, was also sent to the Cepoy camp: "We saw," recalled Karl Kunde, "the CP Opposition forming a group in the camp. It was difficult for us to talk with these people. We even called them the 'fifth column.' "

Kunde encountered a number of Communist authors in the Cepoy camp, among whom were Hans Marchwitza, the author of the book *Sturm auf Essen* (*The Storming of Essen*), and Ludwig

Turek, whose book *Ein Prolet erzählt* (*A Proletarian Recounts*) was widely known among members of the German CP. According to Kunde, Turek adhered to the group of internees who attacked the Hitler-Stalin pact, the Communist party, and the Soviet Union most violently.

Kunde summed up the consequences of the discussions of the Hitler-Stalin pact in the Cepoy camp as follows:

> The majority rejected the Party's viewpoint. One could talk with Machwitza but not at all with Turek. . . . But the Party as such crumbled after the conclusion of the Hitler-Stalin Pact. The major break however was between the Communist and non-Communist internees: everyone was outraged by the pact and one couldn't talk any longer to the Social Democrats and the men of the CP opposition. Even some Communists were unapproachable. We faced them all as a group which defended the view of the CP Germany, namely that the Soviet Union needed to gain time to prepare for the final battle. I stand by my view just as much today as then.[21]

Switzerland: Hans Teubner and the Direction of the "Southern Section"

Hans Teubner, a CP official loyal to the party line, was in Switzerland at the time of the Hitler-Stalin pact. He was born in Aue in 1902, the son of a textile worker, joined the Communist party in 1919, and worked as the editor of Communist newspapers between 1924 and 1927. Between 1927 and 1930, he received a political education at the Lenin School in Moscow. After Hitler seized power, Teubner was arrested and spent two years in the Luckau prison. In 1935, he emigrated to Prague. During the Spanish Civil War, he worked from time to time as an editor at the German Freedom radio station

(*Deutscher Freiheitssender*) in Madrid. He then came to France and was instructed by the emigré CP leadership to go to Zurich in March of 1939. In Switzerland, he directed the "Southern Section," responsible for anti-Fascist activity in the southern part of Germany.

Teubner recorded that many people in Switzerland could not comprehend the Hitler-Stalin pact and that some spoke of "an imminent reconciliation between Bolshevism and Fascism." The situation for the German Communist emigrés was especially difficult:

> Even some Communists were bewildered and couldn't comprehend. While the emigre ate the bread of his charitable host he was told: "Why don't you return to your Stalin who now fraternizes with Hitler? You can return to Germany if Stalin and the Swastika men have settled their differences." That made the emigre's bread taste very bitter. The air which he breathed was poisoned. He needed a good deal of political savvy and a great deal of moral strength to avoid being ground down, to take the offensive and defend the truth.

Like the Communist parties of France and England and the emigré leadership of the CP Germany in Paris, Hans Teubner tried to convince himself and others that the struggle against Fascism was continuing. He wrote an article entitled "The Soviet Union—the bullwark of peace—The rotten Nazi hoax about the Soviet Union/There will never be an alliance between Hitler and Stalin" for the newspaper *Süddeutsche Volksstimme*, which was distributed illegally in Germany. In this article, Teubner wrote—apparently completely mistaking the true nature of the pact—that the Soviet Union would never think "of allying itself with Hitler and his criminal, adventurous policy. . . . The Soviet Union will stand on the side of all those peoples menaced

by Fascism who are determined to defend themselves against
the Fascist attacks. . . . Therefore there can never be an alliance between the Soviets and Hitler."[22]

Teubner did not understand to what degree the pact affected
people in Switzerland: "People gathered in the squares and
streets. 'So it's true' they said. 'Hitler and Stalin have formed
an alliance.' Wherever one went one saw clearly that great
numbers of people were perplexed and had lost their heads
to an indescribable degree. Now it was extremely important
to react quickly. The article quoted above was no longer sufficient."

Teubner wrote yet another exhaustive article, with the significant title, "The policy of the Soviet Union is the policy of
peace/The non-aggression pact is not an alliance or pact of
mutual assistance." In this article, Teubner addressed all of
the attempts of Hitler's system to disarm the working class and
to infect the resistance movement in Germany, with the par-
alyzing thought that "if the Soviet Union has already given up
the struggle against and made common cause with Fascism,
then what are we doing? Our resistance against Hitler is sense-
less."

In an attempt to anticipate this very accurately described
reaction, Teubner tried to play down the pact. In his opinion,
the pact didn't hinder the formation of alliances to oppose the
Fascist aggressors; the Soviet Union was still striving to "negotiate a mutual assistance pact with France and England."
Then Teubner called on the German people to continue the
struggle against Hitler's regime: "Destroy the war machine!
Create and strengthen a united front and the popular front!
Restrain Hitler, regardless of the direction in which he attempts to strike out, to kindle the blaze which will set the
world afire!"[23]

This is the explanation of the director of the Southern

Section in Switzerland. While Hans Teubner was writing this explanation, which was illegally distributed in Germany through *Süddeutsche Volksstimme*, intensive contacts between Hitler's and Stalin's government on the joint action against Poland had been taking place for a long time. The details of the Soviet invasion of Poland were agreed upon on September 17, 1939.

Karl Mewis in Malmö: The Pact With the Devil and the Reorientation of the "Comrades in the Country"

The term "comrades in the country" referred to those party members who were working illegally in Germany. It was used by the emigré leadership of the CP Germany in Paris, by the directors of the various "sections" in the countries bordering on Germany, and by the Comintern leadership in Moscow itself. But what did the Comintern leadership in Moscow know of the comrades in the country? How did they obtain information? Of this we have only one eyewitness account—that of Karl Mewis, who was active in the Swedish port of Malmö and who was called to Moscow only a few weeks after the conclusion of the pact to report to the Comintern leadership about the mood of the comrades in the country.

Karl Mewis was thirty-two years old when, in the summer of 1939, he received the task of maintaining, from his base in Malmö, contact with the Communist groups in Germany and promoting their illegal activities. Born in 1907, Mewis was trained as a mechanic in the railroad's central repair depot in Kassel. In 1923, he joined the KJVD. In 1925, he became chairman of the Federation's organization in

Hesse-Waldeck and a local editor of the Communist newspaper *Neue Arbeiterzeitung*.

Mewis attended the Lenin School in Moscow from 1932 to
1934 and was sent in the late summer of 1934 to perform
illegal tasks in Germany. In the summer of 1935, he returned
to Moscow as a delegate of the German Communists at the
7th Comintern World Congress. Afterwards, he was elected
a candidate member of the Central Committee of the CP Germany at the party's so-called Brussels Conference, which in
fact took place near Moscow. After a brief period of illegal
activity in Hamburg, Mewis traveled via Paris to Spain as a
representative of the CP Germany. In Spain he participated
actively, according to eyewitnesses, in the suppression of independent leftist anti-Fascists. In April 1938, Mewis was
called to Paris, where he joined the emigré leadership of the
CP Germany; in January of 1939, he was appointed one of
seventeen full members of the Central Committee of the German CP at the Bern Conference, which actually took place
at Draveil in the vicinity of Paris. Finally, Mewis was sent
to the Swedish port of Malmö where he learned of the Hitler-
Stalin pact: "To be sure we were somewhat unprepared for this
'pact,' as the treaty was generally called. Moreover we had
been eager to find at least one common ground for action between the Western nations and the Soviet Union against the
main warmonger in Europe." However, Karl Mewis obeyed the
party line and immediately translated it into action. "In particular, I had to help the 'comrades in the country' to reorient
themselves." But there was hardly time for that—before he
could analyze the treaty and its consequences Germany invaded Poland. "It became even more difficult to explain the
peculiarities of this pact with the devil to the 'comrades in
the country,' " he recalled.

Shortly thereafter, he received word that he was to travel to Moscow to report on the situation. He arrived in Moscow with a Swedish passport and met with the top emigré officials of the CP Germany, including Philipp Dengel, Walter Ulbricht and Herbert Wehner, who was known in the Comintern as Kurt Funk. The discussion centered around the situation in Germany and the necessary "tactical orientation." Mewis resided in the Hotel Lux and was also invited by Klement Gottwald, then the Comintern Secretary for Central Europe, to talk. By then, it was November 1939, and he was to report to the Presidium of the Executive Committee of the Communist International.

"Wilhelm Pieck advised me to speak objectively without over-emphasizing any aspect. Naturally I began to get nervous: after all, in addition to Georgij Dimitroff, Jose Diaz and Otto Kuusinen comrades like Andre Marty were present who wouldn't accept anything which wasn't substantiated."

Mewis's report, couched in standard party language, was quite optimistic and explained "that our Party is still a tightly knit organization which is still capable of action despite its extreme decentralization." He then turned to the Hitler-Stalin pact and its effects: "No one seemed surprised that the treaty between the Soviet Union and Nazi Germany was incomprehensible to many comrades. . . . Some of our comrades could not see the reasons which had led to this treaty; some aspects caused them to feel uneasy, while other aspects caused misunderstandings." However, Mewis concluded on an optimistic note; the German Communists felt a deep trust for the Soviet Union and many had recognized "that the Soviet Union could not have acted differently under the present conditions."[24] This was how the Comintern leadership in Moscow learned about the mood of the comrades in the country.

THE PACT AND THE COMMUNISTS
IN FRANCE

The Hitler-Stalin pact had an especially strong and far-reaching impact on the anti-Fascists in France. There were two reasons: First, the CP France was the largest Communist party outside of the Soviet Union and as such was especially affected; second, tens of thousands of anti-Fascist political emigrés from Germany, Italy, many Eastern European countries, and Spain (especially after March 1939) were living in France at the time.

During the period of the Popular Front (1936–1938), the French Communist party had developed from a small organization to a relatively significant political force. The membership had increased tremendously: by the end of 1937, there were 328,000 members, compared with the French Socialist party's 286,000. In the elections in the Spring of 1936, the Communists received 15.3% of all votes, compared with 19.3% for the Socialists. The French Communists were determined defenders of the Republic during this period, and their votes guaranteed Leon Blum's Popular Front government a majority in the parliament in 1936.

At the 18th Party Congress in Moscow in March 1939, Manuilski presented the CP France as a shining example: "The Communist Party of France was the pioneer in the struggle for the anti-Fascist popular front. In five years its membership has grown from 40,000 to the 270,000 of today. While developing the anti-Fascist movement the CP France could find support in the finest revolutionary traditions of its working class and of its people."[25]

Manuilski said these words in March of 1939; by August, this same party was in disarray. After the period of the Popular

Front, the shock of the Hitler-Stalin pact was particularly great for the French Communists—a fact which is reflected in the memoirs of the party's leaders during that period.

Tillon and Ceretti: Hit on the Head With a Hammer Like Cattle in the Slaughterhouse

Charles Tillon, who was forty-three years old in 1939, learned of the Hitler-Stalin pact as did many Frenchmen—while he was on vacation. Tillon, born in Rennes in 1897, worked as a mechanic and then as a sailor. He was one of the instigators of the mutiny of the French fleet in the Black Sea in 1919, which was intended to hinder French support for the Whites in the Russian Civil War. Tillon joined the CP France immediately upon its foundation in December 1920. At first, he was active for the party in the trade unions and was frequently arrested. In the spring of 1931, he was named a member of the Central Committee of the CP France, and in August of 1932, he was made a member of the Politburo. With the victory of the Popular Front in 1936, Tillon became a Communist deputy in the French Assembly. During the Spanish Civil War, he was a member of the General Staff of the International Brigade. He returned to France in March 1939, after the fall of the Republic.

On August 23, 1939, Tillon was spending his vacation with several friends in the little village of Glange in the Departement of Haute-Vienne:

On the afternoon of August 23 we went, as we did every day, to fish for crayfish in a river bordered by old tree stumps. When we returned for supper we heard on the radio that the Soviet Union and Nazi Germany had signed a non-aggression pact. The news seemed so overwhelming, that I stupidly failed to comprehend at first the dramatic consequence which resulted from it. . . . Nevertheless I noticed how I was gradually overcome with fear . . . did the Party leadership really know nothing about it? What was one to think? What would become of our party in the inevitable storm which menaced it?[26]

In contrast to Charles Tillon, who belonged to the leadership of the CP France, Giulio Ceretti was a Comintern official who worked in France under the name Pierre Allard. Ceretti, who was actually Italian, was born in Sesto-Florence in 1903. He was active in the Italian Communist party and then emigrated to France, where he continued his work in Lyon (1927–1929) and from 1929 in Paris, where he worked with the leader of the Italian CP, Palmiro Togliatti, and other Italian emigré Communists. Ceretti was also active in the French anti-Fascist and anti-war movement. He learned of the Hitler-Stalin pact in Paris:

Our struggle against Hitler and Mussolini was not a mere struggle; no, we had it in our blood. The pact signed in the Soviet capital was therefore a rude awakening. It was not as though we were shaken awake but as though we received a heavy blow on the head, like cattle in a slaughterhouse. Perhaps the Soviet comrades did not correctly judge the effects of this measure on the workers' movement and on the party which had created the Popular Front. Devoted activists suddenly did not know what to do, had no political program, no outlook for the future.

Ceretti foresaw that war was now inevitable, and that this war would be unusual. In this dilemma, the party members only had their faith in the Soviet Union: "This was one of those turning points in which our faith, or rather our blind confidence in Socialism, in the fatherland of Socialism, became a decisive element."[27]

Adam Raysky: Explain the Inexplicable

The recollections of Charles Tillon and Giulio Ceretti by no means record isolated impressions; on the contrary, their observations are confirmed by other contemporaries who were active in the CP France or who were adherents of it. In this respect, the reminiscences of Adam Raysky, a journalist and Communist of Polish origin, are of interest. In 1934, Raysky was a delegate at the Congress of the French Communist youth organization in Ivry. From this time he remained close to the leading circles of the CP France, which included Maurice Thorez, Jacques Duclos, and Raymond Guyot, who was then the head of the Communist Youth International. Raysky worked for the party's central newspaper, *L'Humanité*, and frequently met other leaders and adherents of the French CP, such as Andre Marty, Marcel Cachin, or the writer Louis Aragon. Raysky recalled the news of the pact as follows:

In the late evening of August 23, 1939, the news of the signing of a non-aggression pact between Moscow and Berlin resounded like a thunderclap in a humid, stormy sky over a European landscape which was in the grip of extreme tension over a tripartite military alliance between France, England and the Soviet Union.

Impossible! Unbelievable! In the press and on the street these exclamations expressed the general sense of stupefaction, which was also shared by the Communists. One had to realize that Moscow had suddenly renounced signing an agreement with the democratic countries whose military and economic potential could, together with that of the USSR, stop Hitler's expansionist mania.

After the first attack of surprise we had to try to explain the inexplicable. At first our analysis dealt only with the diplomatic consequences of the event; no one dared to imagine

that it would also have ideological repercussions. . . . None
of us would have dreamt that the pact signalled the outbreak
of war, because we were all deeply convinced of the "fatherland of socialism's desire for peace."[28]

Two Swiss who were active Communists for many years—
Paul and Clara Thalmann—also witnessed the effects of the
Hitler-Stalin pact in Paris. Paul Thalmann, who was born in
Basel in 1901 and Clara Ensner, who was seven years younger,
were both active in the CP Switzerland during the 1920s and
had both spent several years in Moscow. They were excluded
from the CP Switzerland in 1928 but remained active socialists.
They went to Spain in 1936 and fought in the militia on the
front in Aragon. Outspoken opponents of Stalinism, they were
consequently arrested in Republican Spain as supposed Fascists. They were freed only when their socialist friends intervened on their behalf.

They went to Paris. Long before the conclusion of the pact,
they "became convinced that Stalin would conclude an alliance
with Hitler." They recalled the pact's effects on the French
Communists:

Nevertheless this immoral pact was also a considerable shock
for us. The masterpiece of authoritarian secret diplomacy
caused endless confusion and then deep bitterness. Panic
broke out in the Communist rank and file who had suspected
nothing. The Communist leaders were unable to act without
directives from Moscow. Up until then Fascism had been
stigmatized as the chief enemy of the working class and of
the proletarian state. What were they to do now? Now the
proletarian state was allied with Fascism and the entire basis
of the Communists' strategy turned upside down. Only the
Party die-hards, who shifted with the changing political winds,
searched frantically for explanations. The Communist bard

Louis Aragon, who penned verse to Stalin, "the sun of nations," wrote in the evening newspaper *Le Soir*: "The warmongers are beaten back, peace is secured." Nevertheless the great majority of the Party members and their fellow travellers remained bewildered and unable to comprehend this alliance. Some of the Communist deputies in parliament rebelled, numerous Communist deputies in the *departements* assemblies and members in municipal councils withdrew from the Party. Many tore up their Party cards.[29]

The Meeting of the Leadership of the CP France in the Rue le Pelletier 44

The difficulties faced by the leadership of the CP France—no directives from Moscow, most of their own cadres on vacation—were, in view of these unforeseen events, enormous. On this fateful day, the French party was headed by Marcel Gitton (1903–1941), who had been a member of the party since its foundation in December 1920. In 1939, he was a member of the Central Committee and the Politburo, as well as a Communist deputy in the French Assembly. At the time of the Hitler-Stalin pact, Gitton was the Politburo member in charge of organizational matters. However, after the pact was announced, he broke with the party and, according to some of his contemporaries, even worked as an informer for the police.

The division among the party's leadership rendered the situation for the CP France even more difficult. Only on August 24 were the most important officials requested to meet in Paris. The meeting took place the following day at No. 44 Rue le Pelletier. Charles Tillon, who was one of the most important participants in this meeting, recalled the following:

On the morning of the 25th I arrived at the headquarters of the CP France in the Rue le Pelletier. Poupon, the affable doorman with one arm, was at his post but more nervous than usual.

"What do you think of it?"

"Hmmm, there will be war, perhaps a world war!"

The members of the Central Committee and the Communist deputies in the French Assembly participated in this meeting. Tillon noted that those present were distinctly uneasy. The discussions, during which two distinct points of view crystallized, apparently did not give the leaders the mandate for which they had hoped. Two CP deputies who were also farmers, Renaud Jean and Sossot, proposed that the CP France send a delegation to the Soviet Embassy requesting that the Soviet Union continue to side with the democratic countries against Nazi Germany.

Maurice Thorez was, according to Tillon, on his high horse, outraged at the critics of the pact. How could anyone presume to interfere in the affairs of the USSR? No one dared to admit that the agreement between Molotov and von Ribbentrop still thoroughly muddled the affairs of the French party. Thorez was content during this meeting with the decision to print the following appeal in the last morning issue of *L'Humanité*: "Stalin was right not to entangle himself alone in a war. Military treaties are still possible if Paris and London want them; however the precondition is that an anti-Communist or anit-Soviet attitude does not take precedence over the interests of peace. Peace is still possible. However if there should be a war against Germany then the Communists will act first and foremost to defend their national security." This was the extent of the party line concluded at this meeting. Charles Tillon commented in his memoirs:

The German-Soviet pact caused a sensation, gripped and yet numbed everyone and broke our hearts. We did not need to disavow ourselves, since we were still determined to wage war against Nazism. If Stalin acted in the interests of the USSR, the land of socialism, then we had the right to act, to the best of our ability, in the interests of the Communist Party of France.[30]

A. Rossi also recorded his impressions of this important meeting, although at that time he was no longer numbered among the leaders of the CP France. A. Rossi was, in reality, Angelo Tasca (1892–1960), who was active in the socialist youth movement of Turin even before the First World War. Tasca was one of the founders of the CP Italy in January of 1921. He was a leading figure in the trade union and agricultural cooperative movements and a delegate of the CP Italy at the 4th World Congress of the Comintern in November 1922.

Later on, Tasca—alias Valle, alias Rienzi—participated in the illegal struggle of the Italian Communists, and in December 1926 began to work for the Comintern in France. Under the party name "Serra," he participated in the 6th World Congress of the Comintern in the Summer of 1928. At that time, he was a member of the Executive Committee of the Comintern, as well as of the two most important organs, the ECCI Presidium and the ECCI Secretariat. Shortly after the 6th World Congress, Tasca ran afoul of the Comintern leadership and of Stalin personally because of the struggle against the "right opportunists" and the heightened struggle against "social Fascism." He was excluded from the party in 1929. He continued to be active in the French Socialist Party but maintained close contacts with the French Communists, about whom he was extremely well informed. Here is his description of the meeting:

The atmosphere of the first meeting on August 25, during which the participants voted on Thorez' motion, was charged and very bad. . . . None other than Renaud Jean, whose coarse candor gave him the reputation of being something of an *enfant terrible*, called out: "What is this supposed to mean? Explain it to us. It means war." Thorez, who didn't know any more than the others, forwarded a few confused hypotheses. Since they were all groping around in the dark, Gustave Sausset, a deputy of the CP France from the Dordogne, suggested that they send a delegation to the Soviet Embassy. The delegation should propose that the Embassy ask the government in Moscow to issue an official statement to the effect that if Hitler should attack Danzig, from which hostilities with the Western democracies would entail, that the Soviet Union would automatically side with those countries which were fighting for their independence.

Thorez, who until then had been cautious and acted as a mediator, reacted with unusual vehemence: "We should not interfere in Russia's foreign affairs!" He continued, shouting at those present: "This suggestion is tantamount to betrayal. We would demonstrate that we have no confidence in Moscow!"

Sausset resigned from the Party the day after the meeting; a deputy of the CP France from the Dordogne, Paul Loubradou, followed his example. They were followed by Jules Fourrier and Marcel Brout, both CP deputies from Paris, and by Gilbert Declerg, a CP deputy from the Departement du Nord.

These five dissidents published an appeal which read: "We continue to affirm the policy of resisting the aggressor and at the same time supporting the democracies which themselves oppose the suppressive regime. We have always opposed genuflecting before Hitler and his regime. We condemn the German-Soviet pact." Moreover, the appeal criticized all those who supported Stalin's policy without regard for French interests.[31]

Marcel Thourel and the Communist
Rank and File in Toulouse

The preceding memoirs dealt primarily with higher party officials in Paris. But how did the pact look to the rank and file party members outside the capital? Marcel Thourel provides us with information in his memoirs, published in 1980.

Thourel, who came from a working-class family, joined the Communist party in 1935. During the Spanish Civil War, he was involved in helping foreign volunteers cross the Spanish border to fight. He returned to the vicinity of Toulouse and learned of the Hitler-Stalin pact during his vacation, which he spent with his Communist friends Maurel and Laroque:

> I had just arrived in Faou-Petit, where I was spending a few days of my vacation when the news reached me out of the blue. Since we had no radio we received the news from two socialists in the next village. We were so amazed that our first reaction was to treat these two men as *provocateurs*. They returned home laughing as though they were pleased to have played a prank on us. Towards evening Maurel, Laroque and I went down to the village; the headlines, which filled the entire page of the newspaper, destroyed any illusion which we might have had. One can imagine the fear and perplexity with which we were filled the following day. In vain I tried to telephone the Party headquarters in Toulouse.
>
> On the following day, August 24, there was no longer any doubt: All of the papers announced that the German-Soviet pact had just been signed. We were utterly crushed. On the 25th we reached Toulouse towards evening. We immediately telephoned or sent telegrams to those Party officials who were on vacation, requesting their immediate return. This was followed by two days of anxious waiting, without the slightest directive from the Party. . . . How should one attempt to explain the inexplicable? The Soviets had, as usual, reached

a decision alone, without informing the leaders of the fraternal parties as a precaution without the slightest interest in the effects of this decision on these parties.

The morale of the few Party officials whom we could gather together in Toulouse, and who vacillated between faith and doubt, was extremely low. . . . In view of such a momentous event we were incapable without directives from the Party, to take even the slightest initiative. How could we have done this anyway, since we were accustomed to receiving instructions from above?

Pourtalet, the Communist deputy in the French Assembly from the Departement Alpes-Maritimes and the representative of the Central Committee, only arrived on the morning of August 27. Marcel Thourel commented, "However Pourtalet seemed to feel as uneasy about the import of the Hitler-Stalin Pact as we did. He had received certain vague directives, but not a clear Party line, since the Party's leadership was not all in the French capital at the time."

Marcel Thourel hastily organized a meeting that evening and invited as many party officials as possible. At the beginning of the meeting he was obliged to accept Marcel Marquie's note of withdrawing from the party. Except for Marquie, the pact did not cause any further spectacular resignations in the Toulouse region, but a good number of the rank and file withdrew from the party.

Pourtalet's speech indicated that the leadership of the CP France was completely surprised by the announcement of the pact. To openly justify the pact in France would be, in Pourtalet's words, tantamount to suicide, since the party would not be able to survive the wave of indignation and accusations with which they were clearly threatened. On the other hand, one had to understand the situation of Stalin and the Soviet leadership; one could not doubt the judgement of the man who resolutely directed the fatherland of all workers. Pourtalet's speech gave the comrades the impression that the party hesitated between unconditional submission to Moscow on the one hand and adherence to the national policy of unity and of the struggle against Fascism on the other.

Marcel Thourel recalled "that for the first time the participants in the meeting did not reach a consensus of opinion. Some of the comrades wavered, which revealed the first crack in the edifice of blind obedience."

The CP chose, as Thourel recalled in his memoirs, a middle path: One should accept the pact as a necessary evil despite the great difficulties which it caused the French Communists. On the other hand, the Hitler-Stalin pact did not signify that the CP France was changing its policy of combating Fascism. In the words of Marcel Thourel: "We were, therefore, to advocate a double line: accept the pact as a temporary compromise but, in view of Hitler's provocations, continue our national policy of defense. This party line was only valid until September 20, the day on which the leadership of the CP France was transferred directly to the Comintern and the new line of the 'imperialist war on both sides' was announced."[32]

The Prohibition of the French Communist Press

While the CP France was in a state of utter confusion, the French government prohibited all Communist newspapers and magazines. In the government's opinion, Stalin's pact with Hitler had rendered the Communists and their sympathizers passive allies of the Nazis and therefore a possible fifth column.

It is ironic that, exactly at the time when the leadership of the CP France had difficulty explaining and justifying the pact to the party's members, it was deprived of the possibility of doing so by the prohibition of the Communist press. The situation was described by Georges Cogniot (1901–1978), a deputy of the Communist party in the French Assembly and the editor-in-chief of *L'Humanité*. He recalled that upon his return from sick leave "the entire editorial staff of the newspaper" met on August 24, as usual, "to assess the situation." On August 25, *L'Humanité* vowed "to stand in the front ranks" in the struggle against the aggressor.[33] The CP France, it was announced in this decisive article, was more than ever the implacable enemy of international Fascism, above all of Nazism. However, as Cogniot observed two days later, all of the newspapers and magazines of the CP France were prohibited. These were, first and foremost *L'Humanité*, with a circulation of 320,000, *Ce Soir*, which sympathized with the Communist party, and 195 newspapers and magazines that were either published by the party or which sympathized with it. Only *La Vie Ouvrière*, the newspaper of the pro-Communist trade union CGT, was allowed to publish for another three weeks, with the result that it became the party's mouthpiece. Homes were searched with increasing intensity, and soon the first people who distributed pamphlets were arrested.

Franz Dahlem records in his memoirs that on August 25 the Paris police forced its way into the editorial offices of *L'Humanité* and confiscated that day's issue, which had just been completed. The CP France succeeded in printing one last, legal issue of *L'Humanité* on August 26. Only part of that issue was confiscated by the police, even though the Communist party had still called on the rank and file to continue the struggle against Hitler: "The unity of all Frenchmen is the duty of the hour. If Hitler tries to do what he says he intends to do, then the French Communists will be in the front ranks of those who defend the independence of nations, of democracy and of France's endangered democratic freedoms." Nevertheless, not only *L'Humanité* but the entire Communist press was soon proscribed. Franz Dahlem described the effects of this prohibition: "The suppression of the press of the French Party which, until then, had been both influential and imposing, had a devastating effect. Even though the French Communists immediately began to publish an illegal edition of *L'Humanité* and a series of pamphlets in spite of all the prohibitions, these only reached a small portion of the masses." The decisive statements of the CP France remained, in Dahlem's opinion, unknown to the populace. Dahlem remarked critically: "It is a fact that the fraternal French party was not sufficiently prepared for these massive blows of the class enemy. . . . Within only a few days the reaction succeeded in isolating to a great degree the CP France from the masses."[34]

The prohibition of the Communist press produced a state of total confusion within the party. The police began to survey the party's headquarters and arrest activists—called "cadres" in party language—who distributed leaflets, with the result that the party began to organize illegal meetings. Many party officials ceased to spend the night in their homes, and the party leadership was largely paralyzed. Jacques Duclos attended to the business of the Secretary General but was very concerned by his loss of all contact with the Communist International.[35]

Giorgio Amendola on the Emigré Leaders of the CP Italy

The state of utter confusion that the Hitler-Stalin pact generated among the leaders of the CP Italy who had emigrated to France was probably almost as great as that among the CP France. Details are provided by Giorgio Amendola, who was one of the emigré leaders of the CP Italy in Paris. Born in 1907, Amendola studied economics at the University of Naples and joined the still illegal Italian Communist party in 1929. At first he was active in the underground; later he spent several years working illegally among Italian emigrés in Paris. He returned to Italy, was arrested in June of 1932, and sentenced; he spent the next five years in exile on the Island of Ponza. Amendola was released in June of 1937 and reached Paris by October of the same year. He wanted to go to Spain immediately, but the leaders of the CP Italy decided that he should stay in Paris and direct a press that would print publications for the Italian emigrés in Paris.

The Great Purge of 1936–1938 also had an effect on the Italian Communists in France: "Vigilance changed into bureaucratic conformism, which until then had been unknown in the daily work of the Italian CP," Amendola recalled. Self-criticism and exclusions from the party were "not infrequently accompanied by pitiful incidents"; fortunately, these stayed within "typical Italian limits." However, these incidents did weaken the party's leaders and endanger the policy of unity against Fascism: "The conclusion of the agreement aggravated the crisis, which had befallen the united movement against Fascism during the years 1936–1938 in the extreme and suddenly isolated the Communists," wrote Amendola. Leading Communists such as Togliatti, Longo, Montagnana, and others were arrested in Paris: "The Communist Party was isolated, the contacts broken, the main exponents were in prison and the split between the Communists and the other anti-Fascists was complete."

Amendola recalled that three groups crystallized among the Italian Communists. One group was prepared to fight on France's side in a war which they viewed as a democratic struggle against Nazism. However, the reaction of the French authorities, especially the arrests and repression to which they were immediately subjected, cooled the democratic fervor of some.

A second group felt it necessary to combat not only German but also Anglo-French imperialism. A third group declared that the Italian Communists should concentrate their efforts in the struggle against Italian Fascism: "Everything for Italy. Everything is directed at Italy. Fascism remains our enemy, even if the Soviet Union treats it differently with the German-Soviet pact."[36]

However, in Amendola's opinion "the comrades were isolated and contacts were lacking, so that it was difficult to undertake anything. Under such conditions it was hard to establish a political position." In addition, a number of party members had either withdrawn from the discussion or even resigned from the party. One of the most important of these was Adami, with the party name of Romano Cocci, who became a member of the Central Committee in 1936 and who was excluded from the party because he opposed the Hitler-Stalin pact.

Even some leading Italian Communists in prison opposed the pact, among whom were Umberto Terracini and Camillo Ravera, who were known throughout the party. Terracini, who was then forty-four years old, was a cofounder of the Italian CP in 1921. Under the name Urbani, he belonged to the ECCI and the ECCI Presidium in Moscow. He was arrested in Italy for illegal activity and sentenced to twenty-two years and nine months in prison. Camillo Ravera also joined the party upon its founding. He was arrested during an illegal stay in Italy in 1930 and sentenced by an extraordinary court. Both Terracini and Ravera had clearly spoken out against the pact, for which they were excluded from the party.

Amendola, in contrast to other historians of the Communist movement, presents these facts openly. It was also rare for the Communist movement that the critics were later readmitted to the party and took part in the continuing struggle:

A good number of them returned to the Party through their partisan work. Many also fought in France in the ranks of the partisans. Even in Italian prisons there were Communists who opposed the German-Soviet pact—I am thinking of a well-known incident which is linked with the names Terracini and Ravera. Both were readmitted, after Togliatti's return, to the Party. Be that as it may, the German-Soviet pact aggravated the existing antagonisms and the confusion within the organized anti-Fascist movement.[37]

Teresa Noce: The Apprehension of the Italian Communists in France

Amendola's remarks are confirmed by Teresa Noce, the wife of Luigi Longo, who was then the head of the CP Italy. Noce (1900–1980), who came from a working-class family, was active in the workers' movement from her earliest youth. She too was a cofounder of the Communist party in 1921 and was known as the "stormy madonna." After a period of illegal activity, she went to the Soviet Union in 1926, where she attended the Lenin School. Upon returning to Italy, she directed the first illegal strike under Mussolini's regime. Noce was a member of the Garibaldi Brigade in the Spanish Civil War and went to Paris after the fall of the Republic, where she worked as a correspondent for the illegal newspaper *L'Unita* in Italy and for the *Voce della Italia* in France.

Her husband, Luigi Longo, was at that time president of the Unione Populare Italiana, an anti-Fascist organization in France with a strong Communist tendency, which attended to the Italian emigrés and to the Italians returning from Spain. The emigré leadership of the CP Italy was, according to Teresa Noce, in a desolate state: "At that time it was impossible to see in which direction the Party was developing. After the Central Committee was disbanded no one even knew who was directing it." In the midst of this situation they received word of the Hitler-Stalin pact:

> Until the day before we had fought so that France and England would ally themselves with the Soviet Union against Hitler. The fact that the so-called democratic governments obviously didn't want to hear about this was considered a betrayal. No one thought it possible that the Soviet Union would sign a pact with Nazi Germany. . . . At first the comrades didn't want to believe the news, and thought that it was a provocation. When we were convinced that it was the truth we looked for reasons. The leadership of the Italian Party, which, as I already mentioned, was not very serious, offered explanations quite late in the game. Some of the comrades had already understood that the pact was the result of the fact that a treaty with France and England had not materialized; other comrades rejected every explanation.

During the week between the conclusion of the pact on August 23 and September 2—the day on which France declared war on Germany—Luigi Longo and many other veterans of the International Brigade considered fighting the Germans in France as they had in Spain. They even spoke of an Italian volunteer regiment in the French army. In the "chaotic situation of those days," as Teresa Noce termed it, some important leaders of the CP, like Romano Cocci (Adami), the Secretary of the Italian Popular Union, opposed the party's policy in protest against the pact and resigned. Despite the confused situation, and although many didn't clearly see the true reasons for the pact, the majority of the Italian emigrés remained, according to Teresa Noce, true to the party.

In this muddled situation, the French police began arresting

CP members: "No sooner had the news of the signing of the Hitler-Stalin Pact begun to spread than the French government began to arrest the anti-Fascists and most of all the Communists—regardless of whether they were French or Italians, Poles or Spanish, Czechs or Jews."

Luigi Longo was also arrested during this wave of arrests.

The comrades were seized one after another. Whoever could not go underground tried to live in someone else's apartment. The Communist press, including the *Voce*, was immediately outlawed. Those of us to whom the underground was not new, did not remain inactive. Even the French Party tried to undertake measures, even though the confusion in their ranks was even greater than in ours. More and more Italians and former volunteers in the International Brigade were arrested in the days that followed. When *L'Humanité* was outlawed the French Communists began to be hunted and we could not expect any more help from them.

Even the most active heads of the CP Italy were arrested, including Pajetta, Eugenio Reale, and Mario Montagnana. Teresa Noce recalled that "every day someone was missing at a meeting. At their homes I encountered their wives and children in tears. It became more and more difficult to assist the families, since the number of those arrested was great and the funds available small. One had to distribute money sparingly and to help those families who were truly destitute."

Given this state of affairs, Teresa Noce was particularly dismayed that a close friend, Leo Valiani, resigned from the party. Nevertheless, Valiani was arrested together with many other Italian anti-Fascists in France when his wife was due to give birth. His wife was young and Teresa Noce was very concerned about her, especially because her parents largely neglected her. "My friendship with Leo had always been warm," she recalled, but "after the signing of the German-Soviet pact we had many discussions." Shortly thereafter she received news that particularly upset her: Valiani had resigned from the party because he could not agree with the Russian-German pact and with the party's position. "I was very bitter about that. Leo and I had been friends and had worked together. I had attended his wedding with Nidia, had looked after his wife, who was due to give birth, and later his child, after his arrest."

Indeed, Teresa recalled many discussions with Leo about the Hitler-Stalin pact. But now she was shaken that he had broken with the party. At first she didn't want to believe the news, but when it proved true she began to cry for the first time in a long while: "The women comrades saw me for the first time as poor, foolish and sensitive. The loss of a comrade and of a dear friend at this point in time and in this way was hard and frightful."[38]

Ilya Ehrenburg's Ulcer

The Soviet writer Ilya Ehrenburg, who in August of 1939 was working in France as a correspondent for the Soviet government newspaper *Izvestija*, recounted an extremely unusual effect of the pact. Ilya Ehrenburg was forty-eight years old at the time; he had been active in the illegal socialist movement in Tsarist Russia even in his youth and was imprisoned for the first time when he was seventeen. However, he succeeded in fleeing Tsarist Russia and in reaching Paris, where he published his first volume of verse in 1910. In the Cafe Rotonde in Paris he became friends with many important artists, among them Picasso, Leger, Apollinaire, and Modigliani. Ehrenburg returned to the Soviet Union during the Civil War from 1917 until 1921, but in 1921 went back to Paris, where he became known particularly for his novel *The Extraordinary Adventures of Julio Jurenito and of His*

Disciples. During the 1920s, he lived partly in the Soviet Union and partly abroad and wrote a number of novels which gained wide recognition. He worked as a war correspondent in Spain for Soviet newspapers during the Civil War, from 1936 until 1938; after the fall of the Republic he worked as a correspondent for the government newspaper *Izvestija* in France and witnessed the effects of the Hitler-Stalin pact in Paris:

"Soon after my return to Paris I heard over the radio that an agreement had been signed in Moscow between the Soviet Union and Germany. . . . My reason made me accept what had happened as inevitable, but my heart rejected it."

Ehrenburg met Suritz, who was then the Soviet Ambassador to Paris:

Suritz showed me the latest copy of the *Pravda*. I saw a photograph: Stalin, Molotov, Ribbentrop and a certain Gauss; all smiling in a satisfied way. (I saw Ribbentrop six years later at Nuremburg where he did not smile: He knew by then that he would be hanged.) Yes I accepted everything but this did not make things easier for me. . . . On that day I fell ill with a sickness that the doctors could not diagnose: For eight months I could not eat and lost over forty pounds. My clothes hung on me as though on a coat-hanger and I looked like a scarecrow. The woman doctor who attended the embassy staff said angrily: "You've no right to let yourself go like that," and wanted me to have an X-ray. It was not worth having one for I knew that the whole thing had happened suddenly: I had read the newspapers, had sat down to lunch and all of a sudden I felt that I could not swallow a morsel of bread. The sickness left me as abruptly as it had begun—from shock: On learning that the Germans had invaded Belgium I started to eat. The doctor solemnly pronounced: "Spasmatic phenomena."

Events followed each other in swift succession. The Soviet-German Non-Aggression Pact was made public on the 24th of August. On 1st September Molotov declared that the pact served the interests of world peace. Nevertheless, two days later Hitler launched the Second World War.[39]

THE EFFECT OF THE PACT ON THE ANTI-FASCISTS IN OTHER COUNTRIES

England: The Reminiscences of Edith Bone and Douglas Hyde

In contrast to the powerful CP France, the Communist party of Great Britain never played an important role. Nevertheless, the Popular Front was able to increase the membership of the British CP from 6,000 in 1934 to 18,000 in the spring of 1939. "Their influence in the trade unions and within the Labour Party has increased," Manuilski attested at the 18th Congress of the CPSU in March of 1939. However, he added the critical comment that "despite this success the Communist Party of England is still the most backward section of the Comintern. It has not succeeded in advancing to the most important groups of the English working class."[40]

Two British Communists, Edith Bone and Douglas Hyde, described their different views of that period. At the time of the pact, Edith Bone was fifty years old. Born in Budapest in 1889, she studied medicine at the University of Budapest and worked in a military hospital in Hungary during the First World War. Shaken by the injustice and misery people suffered during the war, she visited the Soviet Union in 1919 as a member of a Red Cross delegation and became a Bolshevik. During the Russian Civil War, she worked for the Red Army and afterwards as a courier for the Comintern. Still later she worked in the Soviet Trade Mission in Berlin and was simultaneously active for the Comintern. After Hitler seized power in 1933, Edith Bone went to Paris, where she participated in publishing the "Brown Book," and then emigrated to England.

She justified the Hitler-Stalin pact with unusual arguments. Edith Bone judged everything that happened in the Soviet Union during the Stalin era on the basis of her personal experience during the revolutionary days of 1919. As she described in her memoirs: "I was in Petrograd in 1919 and I had read the really absurd allegations made in a section of the British press— gruesome stories about the nationalization of women and the like. Naturally, after that, I distrusted all atrocity stories about the Soviet Union. . . . The pact with Nazi Germany was in my eyes merely a strategem to gain time, during which Russia could prepare and mobilize her forces for the inevitable and imminent show-down."

Although she still defended Soviet policy, she criticized the need to be a "yes man," which was prevalent in the British party at the time: "Nevertheless I found it very difficult myself to conform to Party requirements, because, first of all, I like to tell the truth; secondly, I like to express my opinions—both tastes which were not encouraged in the Party. Nor did I like saying 'Yes' when I meant 'No'—which is one of the things which one definitely had, and has, to learn in the Communist Party."[41]

Edith Bone was offended by "the weakness and the childishly futile policies of the British Communist leaders, who followed and defended every about-face of Soviet policy. This "disgusted me so much that in 1939 I left the Party after twenty years of membership."

Her decisive change of heart came, however, a decade later, in 1949, when she visited her native land, Hungary. She was arrested at the airport in Budapest on October 1, 1949, just before boarding her plane to London. She spent the next seven years in prison and was only freed during the Hungarian uprising of 1956. She was able to return to England with new insights into Communism.

Douglas Hyde, who worked at the newspaper of the British CP, the *Daily Worker*, found it more difficult to defend the Hitler-Stalin pact. For the first time in his career as a Communist, he had serious doubts. Born in Bristol in 1911 to religious parents, Hyde was impressed by the social aspects of Christianity from his earliest youth. However, he became increasingly disillusioned with Christianity's inadequate ideas of reform during the Great Depression. He became active in the International Workers' Aid, a nonpartisan philanthropic organization dominated by the Communist party. Finally, Hyde joined the British CP in 1928; he tried at first to unify Christianity and Communism, but became more and more of a party activist. In 1938, he moved to London and worked as an editor of the *Daily Worker*.

In Hyde's opinion "the Soviet-German Pact . . . did not trouble the trained Marxist at all. . . . The rawer rank and filer may have his doubts and difficulties at such moments but not the well-instructed Marxist." Moreover, some of the intellectuals who joined the British CP during the period of the Popular Front turned away in disgust. A well-known writer who had joined the CP during the anti-Fascist Popular Front wrote to Hyde at the time of the pact: "Your two uncles should contract the plague —Uncle Joe Stalin and Uncle Adolf Hitler."

According to Hyde, most of the CP propagandists asked themselves how to explain the pact to their adherents. Alarmed CP members were subjected to the questions and derision of their fellow workers in the factories. Especially those British who had fought in Spain and whose goal it was to "settle accounts with the Nazis," were very critical of the pact. "For the first time in years," Hyde wrote of himself, he doubted "the correctness of the Party's policy. I felt miserable and demoralized, finding excuses for dropping almost all my political activity."[42]

Nevertheless, after a brief pause Hyde continued working for the party, as did many others. He was especially impressed and convinced by the enthusiasm of the rank and file party members during the Second World War. He became increasingly critical only after 1945, especially because of the development in Eastern Europe. He was outraged by the Communist putsch in Prague in February of 1948 and by the show trials in several Eastern European capitals. He left the CP at the end of the 1940s and returned to Catholicism.

The Pact in an English School

Franz Loeser, the son of German-Jewish parents, was born in Wroclaw (Breslau) in 1924. In 1938, he emigrated to England with his boyhood friend Klaus and attended a school run by Quakers in the village of Otterden in Kent. His teacher, named Dr. Morrison, was a tall, lean man, reserved and taciturn, who hid his feelings behind his moustache. He wore the same suit and tie every day. Loeser recalled that "what impressed me were his tolerance and fairness. Mr. Morrison considered it a matter of course that his students held opinions which were not necessarily his own."

On August 24, 1939, the day on which the Hitler-Stalin pact was announced, the class waited with particular excitement to hear what Mr. Morrison would say. As usual, Mr. Morrison was wearing his grey tweed suit and nondescript tie. Only the occasional twitching of his moustache revealed that the political events of the day disturbed him deeply. "I have brought you four newspapers: the conservative *Times*, the liberal *Manchester Guardian*, the *Tribune*, which is the newspaper of the left-wing of the Labour Party, and *Challenge*, the paper of the Federation of Communist Youth. I shall read the opinions of these four

newspapers on the Non-Aggression Pact aloud and expect that
each of you forms his own opinion."

After Mr. Morrison had read the four commentaries and put
the newspapers aside each of the pupils wanted to express his
opinion. "What should one expect from the lousy Communists?"
shouted one of the boys named Robert Strachey, infuriated and
red in the face. "They preach humanity and pretend to be against
the Fascists, but when the chips are down they knife us in the
back. For me there's no difference between a Communist and
a Fascist."

Mr. Morrison looked at Franz and Klaus. "And what do our
German friends say?" he asked.

Franz Loeser was completely confused. He didn't like Robert
Strachey who was so forward and who had worked himself into
a fury, but what he had said seemed to be true. How could one
make common cause, no, even fraternize with the Nazis? Franz,
uncomprehending, shrugged his shoulders. However, his friend
Klaus, who was a Communist, stood up and declared, "I believe
that Nazi Germany and the Soviet Union will remain arch enemies. But if the Western powers are not prepared to ally themselves with the Soviet Union against Hitler then the USSR has
no other alternative than to protect itself against the Fascists
with every means at its disposal."

Klaus's last words were drowned in the tumult of his class-
mates, who thought that the Soviet Union had betrayed humanity. Mr. Morrison tried to calm the pupils, but they did not want
to be calmed. It began to dawn on many of them that the non-
aggression pact could be the first step toward a war against
England. What would happen then? In the heat of the debate,
one of the pupils named Cathy, with whom Franz Loeser was
smitten, asserted herself. With her voice rising above the din
she said, "You're all really stupid. The lords of creation argue
about everything imaginable except for what is most important:

What are we going to do when war breaks out and the Nazis reduce our school to ashes and rubble with their bombs? We must build an air raid shelter as quickly as possible!"

Franz Loeser continued his discussion in the Free German Youth (*Freie Deutsche Jugend*), which the Communists had organized in England.

We in the Free German Youth believed not only in Marx and Engels. We also believed in Stalin. After Stalin had concluded the Non-Aggression Pact with Hitler and Nazi Germany had unleashed a war against the bourgeois democracies Stalin declared that the war between Hitler and capitalist England was a war between imperialist rivals, an unjust war in which the Soviet Union and the Communists of all countries had to avoid becoming embroiled. The German and the English Communists abided by this. So did the Free German Youth. It was at this point, however, that my faith as a Communist collided with my, admittedly modest, experience in life. I was furious: How could an anti-Fascist stay out of the war? Should I wait until the Fascists had killed my family? Should I watch the Nazis land in England and send me to a concentration camp? What kind of anti-Fascists were these who didn't want to fight against the Fascists?

Franz Loeser and his friend Klaus decided that the logical conclusion was to volunteer for the British Army. As a fresh recruit he took the oath of allegiance in the British Army with conviction, although he did have certain reservations about God and the King. This was followed by six weeks of basic and ten weeks of special training, after which Franz Loeser became an assistant radiologist in the Royal Army Medical Corps. In 1945, he was sent as a British soldier to Hiroshima, where he was deeply shocked. He later studied philosophy at the University of Minnesota, witnessed McCarthyism in the early 1950s, and continued his studies at the University of Manchester. In 1957, he moved to East Germany, where he was a professor of ethics. Finally, in 1983, deeply disillusioned, he returned to the West.[43]

Italy: Antonio Pesenti
in the Prison of Fossano

The fact that many Italian Communists—in emigration in France as well as in Italian prisons—were filled with doubts about the pact and that some even left the party was mentioned earlier in the reminiscences of Giorgio Amendola. Naturally, there were also Italian Communists who immediately defended the pact. A particularly interesting case of this was the twenty-nine-year-old Antonio Pesenti, who was in an Italian prison at the time of the pact and who completed his transformation from a socialist to a Communist at this time.

Antonio Pesenti was born in Verona in 1910 and grew up in an anti-Fascist intellectual family. He studied in Padua and then spent three years, from 1931 to 1934, in Vienna, Bern, Paris, and London. During his stay abroad, he came into contact with Soviet diplomats but remained a socialist. After he returned to Italy, he was appointed professor at the University of Sassari in December 1934, but was arrested at the end of 1935. During his several years in the prison of Fossano he became a Communist, for which the Hitler-Stalin pact provided the decisive impetus. Pesenti recalled: "At the end of August, 1939 came the news of the German-Soviet Non-Aggression Pact which was doubtless a bitter pill for all of us prisoners. . . . The problem was assessed and discussed in the dormitories."

Although Pesenti regretted the German-Soviet treaty, he was convinced that, in the final analysis, it was right and he tried to explain this to the other prisoners: "However at that time this view provoked not a few discussions among us. Nevertheless my conviction was so strong that I wanted to declare my position openly. I felt obliged to intervene in this vehement discussion which had broken out in the dormitory and in which the advocates of 'justice and freedom' branded the Pact as a 'treason', even though the Communists themselves had their doubts."[44]

Pesenti wrote a letter informing everyone that he now considered himself a true Communist and requested the party to take official note of the fact.

Hungary: Zoltan Vas in the Prison of Budapest

To the Hungarian Communist Zoltan Vas, the Hitler-Stalin pact began as an "ideological muddle" and ended in an unusual manner with his release from prison and journey to the Soviet Union.

Zoltan Vas (1903–1982) came from a bourgeois family and began to participate in the illegal Communist youth movement at the age of sixteen. He was arrested at eighteen and was sent to the Soviet Union in an exchange of prisoners. There he spent three years, returning to Hungary in 1924 to work illegally. One year later, Vas was again arrested and sentenced to fifteen years in prison. Of the news of the Hitler-Stalin pact he wrote: "I learned of the event when, after ending my one hour walk in the prison yard, a pro-Fascist officer addressed me: 'Yesterday Hitler and Stalin signed a pact; from now on they're political friends.' "

Zoltan Vas was not permitted to receive any newspapers and only occasionally received an odd issue that was smuggled in.

He had not heard anything of the Hitler-Stalin pact, so he could not really understand what the officer meant. The latter continued, however, and explained that the two Foreign Ministers, von Ribbentrop and Molotov, had signed a treaty.

> I hardly wanted to believe the news, since the prison guards were always trying to "save souls": The whole time I was subjected to a variety of attempts to convince me to renounce Communism. Before then they had belabored me repeatedly with untruths. But the prison officer showed me the photograph which the Hungarian newspaper had taken from the *Pravda* showing Molotov and von Ribbentrop in Moscow signing the treaty. In the middle of the picture was Stalin.
>
> "Incredible" said I. Nevertheless I began to adapt to comprehending the incomprehensible. During the course of my Communist activity, together with Communists around the world and even now in prison, I had firmly believed that what is good and advantageous for the Soviet Union is unconditionally good for the adherents of Communism, good for all Communist parties. . . . This basic attitude helped me now to comprehend the news given me by this Fascist officer.

Vas also believed that the Soviet Union was trying to gain time. He too hoped that the Communists' struggle against Fascism would continue. However, when he learned at the end of September 1939 that the Soviet Union had signed a friendship and border treaty with Germany he was "speechless," as he wrote in his memoirs. "I too lapsed into ideological confusion —I, the imprisoned Communist. I couldn't dream that this pact would enable me to go as a free man with Rakosi in November, 1940 to the Soviet Union."[45]

Indeed, an agreement was reached in the autumn of 1940 between the Horthy government in Hungary and the Soviet government permitting a number of imprisoned Hungarian Com-

munists to travel to the Soviet Union. In exchange, the Soviet
Union gave the Hungarians several banners captured by the
Tsarist troops which crushed the Hungarian uprising of 1848.

Zoltan Vas arrived in the Soviet Union in the autumn of 1940
and returned to Hungary in 1944, where he became mayor of
Budapest and head of the state planning agency. In 1945, he
was appointed to the Central Committee of the Hungarian party
and was a member of the Politburo from 1948 until 1953. After
Stalin's death, he sided with the reformers and supported Imre
Nagy and the Hungarian uprising of 1956. When the uprising
was crushed, Vas and Nagy were deported to Rumania. Vas
only succeeded in returning to Budapest in 1958. He did not
return to the party but lived a completely secluded life as a
nonpartisan writer until his death in 1982.

The Yugoslav Communists: Yes to the Pact, But the Struggle Continues

In 1939, the head of the illegal Communist party of Yugoslavia
was Josip Broz, known as Tito, who was forty-seven years old
at the time. Born in 1892 to a Croatian peasant family, Tito was
trained as a metal worker. In March 1915, during the First
World War, Tito was taken prisoner by the Russians and was
only freed during the Russian Revolution of 1917. He joined
the CP Yugoslavia in September of 1920 and was active in the
metal workers' union in Croatia. He was arrested and imprisoned
from the end of 1928 until 1934. In July of 1934, he was
appointed to the Central Committee and in December of the
same year to the Politburo of the Yugoslav party. After becoming
General Secretary, he transferred the leadership of the Yugoslav
party from abroad to Yugoslavia. Tito was in Moscow twice in
1938 and 1939, where he sensed a strong distrust of Yugoslav

Communists as a result of the purges. He returned to Yugoslavia in March of 1939.

> Then came August 1939, the Soviet-German pact. We accepted the pact like disciplined Communists, considering it necessary for the security of the Soviet Union, at that time the only Socialist State in the world. We were ignorant at the time of its secret clauses, countenancing Soviet interference in the rights of other nations, especially small ones. But the Soviet-German pact did not for a moment weaken our vigilance in preparing for the defence of the homeland in the event of attack, nor did it alter our Party line in the general struggle against German and Italian imperialism.[46]

The fundamental concept of "yes to the pact while continuing the struggle against German Fascism" is also expressed in the memoirs of Milovan Djilas and Svetozar Vukmanovic.

In 1939, the twenty-eight-year-old Milovan Djilas was already a leader of the CP Yugoslavia. At the time of the Hitler-Stalin pact he was a member of the Central Committee and of the Politburo. Although he later became one of the harshest critics of dictatorial Communism, Djilas still adhered to Stalin's policy in 1939. As he explained in his memoirs, which were published in 1973, he had approved of the pact with reservations: "I actually approved of the Soviet-German Pact, as did most of the leading Communists, with only a few misgivings. We had already trained ourselves to have absolute confidence in the Soviet Union and in the decisions of its government." However, Djilas understood that the pact paved the way to war and was closely linked with the fate of Poland:

> The news of the Soviet-German Pact was carried in the morning papers. Some intellectual leftist friends said that it could have both positive and negative results. I attacked them

violently. I could see only positive results emerging for the Soviet Union, and thus for us Communists too. I knew that an attack on Poland was inevitable, and that the Western powers would respond with a declaration of war. This, I thought, would create an ideal opportunity for the Soviet Union to spread socialism at the expense of the two warring sides.[47]

Djilas may have been more stunned in reality than he recorded in his memoirs. At least this was the impression of Svetozar Vukmanovic-Tempo, who experienced the Hitler-Stalin pact together with Djilas. Svetozar Vukmanovic—Tempo was his party name—was twenty-seven years old in 1939. Like Djilas, he was born in Montenegro. He studied law at the University of Belgrade, was active in the Communist student movement, and in 1932 became a member of the illegal CP Yugoslavia. In 1935, he passed the bar examination, but instead of practicing law, worked full-time for the illegal Communist party. He describes in his memoirs that he sometimes had reservations; he doubted, for example, that Trotsky really was an "imperialist agent." However, he tirelessly continued his party work. He was repeatedly arrested and imprisoned, and was released from prison for the last time in July of 1939. At the time of the Hitler-Stalin pact, he was a member of the regional committee of the Communist party in Serbia. Vukmanovic recalled the following:

One day in August, 1939 I encountered Djilas in a state of extreme excitement. The German-Soviet Non-Aggression Pact had just been publicized. Djilas walked excitedly back and forth in his room and tried to understand clearly what meaning this development would have for maintaining our own party. After a while he said: "This has no influence at all on our resolve to defend our homeland; nothing can make us swerve from this path!" I was deeply impressed at the way he stuck to his bold approach in this new and complicated situation. [48]

However, there is no doubt that the Yugoslav Communists encountered serious personal and political-psychological problems with the pact. Vilko Vinterhalter, who was also active in the CP Yugoslavia at the time and who also later wrote a biography of Tito, recalled in his book published in 1969 that "even today, thirty years later, one still has difficulty presenting one's own thoughts and feelings about certain manifestations of the international workers' movement." All of the activists of the Communist movement encountered in the pact the limit "up to which one can and must understand things rationally and up to which these things are logically motivated." In Vinterhalter's opinion, the pact impeded their initiative "and the search for their own solutions, which are always necessary." [49]

Jiri Pelikan and the Critical Students of Prague

Czechoslovakia was occupied by German troops in March of 1939 and was officially called the "Protectorate of Bohemia and Moravia." Five months later, the Hitler-Stalin pact was signed—a tragic development, especially for the Communists in Czechoslovakia.

Jiri Pelikan, who was born in 1923 in the small Czech town of Olomuc (Olmütz), had just joined the illegal Communist party in 1939. Jiri's brother, who was seven years older, studied medicine; he had joined the Communist party in 1936 and was Jiri's model: "When you have doubts," he told Jiri, "then trust the Soviet Union and the party. They know what to do."

After the treaty of Munich in September 1938, the fifteen-year-old Jiri, like many of this friends, felt a mixture of powerlessness and the burning desire to do something. Then, only a few months later, in March of 1939, Czechoslovakia was occupied.

Jiri's brother was already active in the Communist underground; he arranged for the sixteen-year-old Jiri to spend his vacation in a youth camp on Lake Rendlicek, which was secretly organized and run by the Communist party. "We attended courses on Marxism, the struggle against Fascism, dialectical materialism and the Soviet Union," recalled Jiri. "In the evening we sang revolutionary songs around a camp fire, sang the songs of Soviet partisans and recited verse." Some of the young people were prepared for the underground by the older comrades. Shortly thereafter, Jiri Pelikan joined the illegal Communist party of Czechoslovakia:

A friend, who identified himself as the Party Secretary in our town, immediately assembled us. Were we prepared to distribute illegal pamphlets and the Party newspaper and to agitate in the high schools? We were prepared. He instructed us in the rules of underground activity and, in view of our participation in illegal work, allowed us to join the Communist Party without a trial period. . . . From that day on we belonged to the great—not only Czech but international—family of the Communist movement. That was an extraordinary event for me and the beginning of a double life: on the one hand school and the behavior of an average pupil which was recommended by the Party; on the other hand clandestine activities in the evening or at night and duties which gave me the sense of serving a great cause. We were presented with an ideal: Soviet society, which did not suffer from the exploitation of man by man, from unemployment and injustice. . . . We were the motor of history!

But this, Pelikan recalled, was only one side of the coin, for now they were confronted with something completely new: the Hitler-Stalin pact.

It was as though we had been deafened by the thunderclap of the Non-Aggression Pact between Germany and the Soviet Union. In our view the Soviet Union was the arch enemy of Nazi Germany—how, therefore, were we to interpret such a pact? I can clearly recall many sleepless nights spent talking with my brother and other comrades who explained to us that the Soviet Union is threatened with isolation by the Western Allies. France and Great Britain do not really want to sign an agreement with the USSR. On the contrary, they want Germany to attack the Soviet Union and destroy it.

The arguments of Jiri's brother were even more interesting:

My brother repeated again and again: "You have to understand us. In a revolution there are always advances and set-backs. A particular set-back may appear at first to be a defeat, but reveals itself later as a victory. Since the Soviet Union is the only socialist country in the world it had to hinder this encirclement by concluding the pact with Hitler, just as Lenin once did in Brest-Litovsk with the German Kaiser: He made use of the contradictions between the capitalist countries to save socialism and to unleash a movement which would eventually turn to his advantage."

"Yes, but how should I explain that to my schoolmates who say 'Listen, Stalin has allied himself with Hitler and you, who sympathize with the Communists, have betrayed us. Now Moscow has abandoned Czechoslovakia."

Pelikan tried to explain the tactical considerations behind the pact, although, as he later wrote, these discussions didn't rid him of all of his own doubts. It wasn't just the pact, but that which he heard from Moscow: "Radio Moscow's Czech broadcasts praised, to our great amazement, the achievements of Soviet agriculture, and the increase in the number of hogs and agricultural machinery while all around the Gestapo was arresting comrades and patriots, was torturing and murdering. About that, however, Radio Moscow was silent—not a word of criticism of Hitler's regime."[50]

The consternation of the Czech Communists, whose country had been occupied by German troops only few months before, is described in other memoirs. Gusta Fucikowa, the widow of Julius Fucik, known as Julek, describes how she learned of the pact in Plzen (Pilsen):

> In August of 1939 the Soviet Union concluded a Non-Aggression Pact with Nazi Germany. People were bewildered. We too were unprepared for the event. Many people came to Julek: the mayor, our tenant, a railroad worker who had been expelled from Slovakia and several workers who were employed in Plzen. They all complained that "the Russians have left us in the lurch! We only trusted them, and placed all our hope in them, that they would free us from Hitler. Instead they befriend him, our arch enemy!"

Gusta Fucikowa, whose memoirs were published in Czechoslovakia and later in East Berlin, presented Julek as courageous and loyal to the party: "Julek didn't vacillate. He had unshakeable faith in the Soviet Union. He patiently explained the treacherous policies and the anti-Soviet attitude of the Western powers to the people. He assured each one that the Soviet Union would never leave our people in the lurch."[51]

Belgium: Leopold Trepper and the "Red Orchestra"

Leopold Trepper, who was later known as the legendary head of the "Red Orchestra," worked in Belgium at the time for Soviet intelligence. Born in Poland, he went as a boy to Palestine, where he joined the CP in 1925. He was arrested several times and was later the Secretary of the CP organization in Haifa. In 1932, Trepper went to the Soviet Union, where he was trained at the Communist University of the Peoples of the West. He attended the famous 7th Congress of the Communist International from July 25 until August 8, 1935, and was appointed to work in the headquarters of Soviet military intelligence (located at 19 Znamenskaya Street). In December 1936, military intelligence sent him to Antwerp and, at the beginning of 1937, to Paris. In the summer of 1937, Trepper returned to Moscow and was instructed to create an intelligence center in Brussels under the cover of an import-export firm. This firm was in fact incorporated in 1938 as The Foreign Excellent Trench Coat Co. At the time, Trepper resided in an unpretentious apartment at 117 Avenue Bols in Brussels. It was here that he experienced the first knowledge of the Hitler-Stalin pact: "I could see how profoundly this policy had disoriented the Belgian Communist militants. Some were torn, but resigned themselves; others, in despair, left the party."

Trepper recorded his own views and those of his friends in the Red Orchestra, which he was forming:

During this great upheaval, in which long-established beliefs and ideals were being contradicted by actions, we who formed the initial nucleus of the Red Orchestra clung to a single idea. In spite of all Stalin's contortions, war with Germany was inevitable. This compass in the storm saved us from foundering. We had to keep going, no matter what happened. We might have inner conflicts, but we had set a mission for ourselves, and we did not have the right to abandon it.

However, it was not easy to execute this plan—Trepper was terribly shocked to learn that Moscow was apparently no longer interested in his intelligence activity directed against Nazi Germany:

At the end of 1939, I received several communications that showed me the new directors of the center were no longer interested in the Red Orchestra. Not only had the center stopped sending the promised emissaries to the branches of *Au Roi du Caoutchouc* [the Communist front organization], but several dispatches urgently requested me to send Alamo and Kent back to Moscow, and Leo Grossvogel to the United States. I too was asked to return to Moscow.[52]

Sweden: The Controversy in the Loka Brunn Internment Camp

The memoirs previously quoted deal almost exclusively with the first reactions to the pact. In fact, the discussions, problems, and contradictions lasted for months. Proof of this is found in the memoir of Ruth Seydewitz who, in the spring of 1940, was in the Loka Brunn internment camp in Sweden together with other emigrés—mostly German and Austrian anti-Fascists—

who had fled to Sweden from Norway and Denmark as they were occupied by the Nazis.

Ruth Seydewitz was born in 1905 in Oppeln as Ruth Lewinski. She studied art history and philosophy at the University of Breslau (Wroclaw), joined the Social Democratic party (SPD) in 1923, and moved to Vienna, where she became a seamstress in order to earn a living. Later, she traveled to Germany, where she belonged to the left wing of the Social Democratic party; for a time, she was even influenced by the writings of Leon Trotsky. In 1931, she joined the Social Workers' party (SAP), of which Max Seydewitz, her future husband, was a leader. After Hitler seized power, she fled to Czechoslovakia, where, in 1934, her husband became a secret member of the Communist party, even though he outwardly remained a leader of the SAP. After the treaty of Munich in the autumn of 1938, Max and Ruth Seydewitz went to Norway; for the first few days they lived with Willy Brandt in Oslo until they found their own quarters. When Hitler attacked Norway on April 9, 1940, they found themselves in the grotesque situation of fleeing from German troops while the Soviet press was justifying Hitler's invasion of Norway and Denmark. After a hair-raising journey, they crossed the Swedish border and were interned in the Loka Brunn camp in Darlane. It was here that they heard discussions about the Hitler-Stalin pact.

"Through the open window I could hear people talking on the bench below," Ruth Seydewitz recalled.

The most vehement discussions were about the German-Soviet Non-Aggression Pact. Some argued about whether or not the Soviet Union's proposal to the governments of England and France to conclude a treaty with the Soviet Union in order to form a strong, defensive block against Nazi Germany had been in earnest. Others said that it was wrong to maintain that

England and France had not really intended to negotiate seriously with the Soviet Union. Others disagreed, pointing to the fact that the Western powers had only sent second or third rate negotiators to Moscow. Certain emigrés found it outrageous that some Communists believed that England and France had used the negotiations with the USSR as an unfair ploy to gain time to negotiate secretly with Hitler.

Ruth Seydewitz reported the reaction of some loyal Austrian Communists with apparent approval:

"Don't you understand anything at all?" a few Austrian Communists said in excitement. "Are you such dolts that you don't understand that the Soviet Union is expecting the Nazis to attack and must defend itself? The USSR must gain time— that's the reason!" And so it went back and forth, and more than one didn't know in the heat of the debate who was right.[53]

Walther Bringolf in Switzerland: "The Pact Means Abandoning Poland"

One of the most remarkable reactions to the Hitler-Stalin pact is that of Walther Bringolf (1895–1981), once a leading Swiss Communist who as early as 1939 had switched to the Social Democratic party.

Walther Bringolf had been a delegate at the 2nd World Congress of the Comintern in Moscow in the summer of 1920 and was one of the founding members of the CP Switzerland in March 1921. In 1925, he was elected to the Swiss parliament as a Communist delegate from Schaffhausen. At the end of the 1920s, he joined the CP opposition; he was the mayor, or *Stadtpräsident*, of Schaffhausen for many years, and in the mid-1930s he and his Communist party friends joined the Swiss Socialist party.

From 1945 to 1952, Bringolf was the leader of the Socialist representatives in the Swiss parliament, and from 1952 until 1962, Chairman of the Swiss Socialist party.

In the summer of 1939, Walther Bringolf was in Paris, where he met Willi Münzenberg, who had already broken with the Communist party and who was publishing his own journal, *Die Zukunft* (*The Future*). From Paris he journeyed to Switzerland; in Basel he read the special issue of the *Nationalzeitung* with the headline "Conclusion of a German-Russian Non-Aggression Pact Near." He traveled on to Zurich, where he met with the president of the Swiss Social Democratic party, Hans Oprecht, and other party leaders to discuss the situation.

Immediately thereafter, Walther Bringolf wrote his commentary, which was printed in the Social Democratic newspaper *Volksrecht* on August 22, 1939, one day *before* the pact was signed. Under the headline "Agreement Berlin-Moscow," Bringolf wrote that this news was very grave for the entire working class and for all who opposed Fascism, since it would disillusion them all:

The text of the Non-Aggression Pact is, at the moment, not yet known. The pact means—in this we shouldn't deceive ourselves for an instant—that Poland is abandoned. Even if the Non-Aggression Pact should only mean that the Soviet Union remains neutral in a European war, then Poland has been delivered up to the German invasion. . . . Hitler has made his final preparations for this war. The German army is ready to march against Poland. . . . Switzerland's position is made extremely difficult by this new development.

Nevertheless not for an instant should we nor may we lose our faith in the forces of freedom in Europe and especially in our own strength. Insiders knew that Russia's help was always questionable. If Russia jumps off and is no longer interested in the struggle against the Nazis' and the Italian Fascists' hunger for power and conquest, then there remains nothing for us to do but to take note of this. We do this with a feeling of disappointment, of outrage, and of bitterness. Not for an instant, however, may we transform this into defeatism or into a loss of confidence in our own strength. Europe's forces of freedom have a mission to fulfil and the working people of Switzerland may not abandon its role.[54]

The Concerns of Jules Humbert-Droz, the Head of the CP Switzerland

Jules Humbert-Droz, who was then Political Secretary of the CP Switzerland, was already full of doubts about Moscow's Stalinist policy when he received news of the Hitler-Stalin pact.

Jules Humbert-Droz (1891–1971) was originally a Protestant clergyman who, as a convinced pacifist, refused to serve in World War I. He belonged to the left wing of the Socialist party of Switzerland and went to Moscow as early as 1920, where he frequently met Lenin. In March of 1921, he helped found the CP Switzerland. Only a few weeks later, at the 3rd Congress of the Comintern in Moscow from June 22 until July 12, 1921, Humbert-Droz was elected Secretary of the Executive Committee of the Communist International. He traveled several times under various assumed names to the Communist party of France and to Italy, Spain, and South America as an emissary of the Comintern. In the summer of 1924, he was appointed to the Organizational Office in the Comintern headquarters and in November 1926 to the Political Secretariat. The spread of the left-sectarian line in the Comintern at the end of 1928 led to a personal attack by Stalin, and Humbert-Droz was relieved of all Comintern duties. He performed self-criticism, returned to Switzerland, and continued for several years as a member of the Politburo and as the Political Secretary of the Swiss party.

Humbert-Droz learned of the Hitler-Stalin pact with Marino Bodenmann, who was also a cofounder of the CP Switzerland. Bodenmann was appointed to the Politburo in the mid-1920s, was elected a Communist representative to the Swiss parliament in 1939, and was at the same time editor of the party's newspaper *Freiheit*, published in Basel. Jules Humbert-Droz recalled:

> I received the news (of the Non-Aggression Pact) on August 24, 1939 at 6:00 A.M. from Marino Bodenmann, who was then editor of the *Freiheit* in Basel and who roused me from my sleep with his message. My first reaction was, verbatim, "Shit! That's exactly what we needed!" What were we to do? Naturally try to explain that the USSR wanted to stay out of war and preserve peace for its people. And that's just what we did. . . . Nevertheless I found Stalin's about face a betrayal of our entire policy of combatting Fascism and of fighting for peace. Because it was evident that Hitler wanted to be certain that he would not be disturbed in the East before he started a war. Germany could not fight on two fronts and the Non-Aggression Pact secured him, if not direct military aid, then at least the benevolent neutrality of the USSR and to some extent supplies which Germany needed. With this pact Stalin promised not to help any power which could attack Nazi Germany. . . . This pact was only the beginning of further betrayals: The invasion of Poland by the Red Army and the partitioning of that country with Hitler; the aggression against Estonia, Lithuania and Latvia and their annexation to the USSR even though Lenin had recognized their independence. . . . Once again I remained at my post as the Chairman of the Communist Party of Switzerland. . . . Our task was to save the Soviet Union and freedom in the world—in spite of Stalin and his policy.[55]

In a long interview, Humbert-Droz's inner conflict was confirmed by his wife Jenny, who had also been politically active throughout her life. Both she and her husband had believed official Communist statements, even during the period of the Moscow show trials, albeit with some criticism. At the same time, they hoped, as did many other Communists at that time, for a turn to the better: "We were convinced that there would be a shift at some time and then everything would be on the right track. My husband and I remained in the CP as long as possible, until we were excluded from it." Did this occur with a divided conscience? Jenny Humbert-Droz answered that her conscience was "even more divided than in 1939 when the pact between Hitler and Stalin was concluded. "At that time we felt that something wasn't right; we were very much in doubt, but we kept on, even though we were excluded from all activities and were very isolated in the Party."[56]

The Mysterious Radio Operator of "La Taupiniere"

La Taupiniere ("the mole's hill") was in the Alps, 1,200 meters above sea level, in the French part of Switzerland, not far from the village of Caux. It was a renovated farm house, cut off from everything else. The back half of the house was a stable for a dozen cows, above which was a hayloft. The front half comprised three rooms. Far below one could see Montreux and Lake Geneva. Ahead were the French Alps, 3,000 meters high. The house was so cut off that one had to park one's car half a kilometer away; thereafter, only a narrow, grassy, almost hidden path led to La Taupiniere. Here was the radio equipment necessary to maintain contact with Moscow, more then 2,000 kilometers away.

The equipment was well hidden in a closet with drawers. Beneath the lowest was a hollow space covered with planks. The bottom plank could be removed, and inside the radio equipment was installed so that it didn't have to be withdrawn in order to operate it. The two holes for the banana pins were covered with wooden plugs which looked like knotholes from the outside.

Ruth Werner, who was thirty-one years old at the time, arrived in La Taupiniere in October of 1938. Born in Berlin, she had been trained to run a book store. She joined the CP Germany in May 1926, and was soon used for special missions. From 1930 until 1932, she was in China, where she learned Chinese and was trained in the methods of undercover work by the famous Soviet spy Richard Sorge. At the beginning of 1933, she returned to the Soviet Union, where she was trained in a "school for emissaries" for her subsequent activity. (In the Eastern bloc countries the word "spy" is always used for the enemy; one's own spies are called "emissaries.") Ruth Werner arrived in China in April of 1934, having traveled via Prague and Trieste. This time she conducted intelligence activity in Mukden, Shanghai, and Peking. She returned to Moscow in 1935 and was instructed to learn Polish. She arrived in Warsaw in February 1936 and in Gdansk (Danzig) at the end of the same year. In both cities she installed radio equipment and transmitted messages to Moscow.

Ruth Werner returned to the Soviet Union in the spring of 1938; to judge by her memoirs, which were published in East Germany, she noticed nothing of the Great Purge. Instead, she describes her promotion from captain to major, which occurred at that time, and her award of the Order of the Red Banner by Kalinin, who was then head of State. Her next job was to travel to England and then to Switzerland for a period as "radio broadcaster."

She met a contact in London: "I only told him what was absolutely necessary. My political work was directed against Nazi Germany. I needed one or two comrades who had proven themselves courageous and dependable during the Spanish Civil War and who were prepared to go to Germany to perform illegal and even dangerous work. I didn't even mention the Soviet Union." Werner's last remark would later prove to be significant.

With the help of her contact, she found two young and dependable comrades. One of these was Alexander Foote, who soon received the alias "Jim" and whom she described as one who "understood quickly and posed reasonable questions. He seemed resourceful and clever, which was important for our work, for he could react quickly to new and unexpected situations. He must have proven in Spain that he was a good and courageous fighter, for otherwise he wouldn't have been recommended for this job. . . . Jim made a good impression on me."

However, Werner remarked critically that Jim valued good food and drink too highly, and that he sometimes burst into a torrent of cynicism. However, because this was only directed at political opponents, it didn't seem too dangerous. Jim was in his early 30s, tall, with reddish blond hair, fair eye lashes, fair skin, and blue eyes. He was handsome and well mannered. His task was to keep his eyes and ears open in Munich, to become acquainted with Nazis, and, if possible, to get to know people who worked in the Messerschmidt aircraft factory.

The second man—also an English Communist—was a twenty-five-year-old named Len. He had thick, brown hair, heavy eyebrows, and bright, greenish brown eyes. He was slim, but strong and muscular. Ruth Werner observed critically that he made a somewhat youthful and raw impression, but that, in contrast to Jim, he was indifferent to the material side of life. Len agreed enthusiastically when he learned that he had been selected for a dangerous job in Nazi Germany. He was to live in Frankfurt/Main and attempt to get to know people who worked at IG Farben. Both Jim and Len were not only to gather information, but to investigate the possibility of sabotage and prepare other acts of active resistance and, they assumed, carry them out at the proper time.

The last member, Hermann, joined the group in April of 1939. He was to move to Fribourg in the western part of Switzerland. For the first few months, he was to do very little but find suitable lodgings where he could install a second radio station. He was a German Communist and a veteran of the Spanish Civil War, and Werner considered him to be completely reliable. The only disadvantage was that he had a Finnish passport but could not speak a word of the language.

In La Taupiniere, Ruth Werner succeeded in beginning her work relatively quickly. The contact with Moscow was good and the possibility of hiding things excellent. A door in the hallway of the second story led directly to the hayloft. The farmer withdrew his hay from the loft door on the outside, but never reached the inner door to which Ruth Werner had the only key. She hid what was secret in the hay.

Werner soon made acquaintances in Geneva. Among them were an Englishman who had an important position at the League of Nations in Geneva and a woman who was the chief librarian of the League of Nations, who also knew many people. Having already learned English, Russian, Polish, and Chinese, Werner now began to study French. She completely concentrated on the struggle against Nazi Germany, which involved not only collecting information but also preparing acts of sabotage and supporting anti-Fascist organizations.

This was the situation when Werner heard the news of the Hitler-Stalin pact. She had met Hermann in Zurich: "The Non-Aggression Pact cost us a lot of reflection. We understood that the Western powers hoped that Nazi Germany and the Communist Soviet Union would destroy each other leaving them laughing on the sidelines. That was to be avoided. But one had to repress one's feelings and rely on logic in order to react properly."[57] This is the extent of Ruth Werner's cautious commentary, which is included in her memoirs published in East Germany.

Werner's closest colleague, "Jim" (Alexander Foote), later mentioned her in his own memoirs as a traitor who broke with the system and with the Soviet Union. Moreover, from Jim's point of view, the effect of the pact on the "broadcaster of La Taupiniere" was much greater than she would have others believe. Having worked for several years against Nazi Germany, Jim was instructed to go to Paris after the liberation of the city, and in January 1945 was recalled to Moscow on the first Soviet plane. In Moscow he was subjected to suspicious and degrading interrogations, which lasted for months, before those in charge trusted him. He received additional intelligence training in the Soviet Union and, at the beginning of 1947, was instructed to pose as a German and reside in Germany for a while. He was then to travel to Argentina and establish an intelligence network directed against the United States.

Jim's two-year sojourn in the Soviet Union succeeded in curing him of all of his pro-Soviet illusions; he decided, therefore, to accept his new assignment and then defect at the appropriate time. Jim, or rather Alexander Foote, first settled in East Berlin as he had been instructed and prepared to begin his assignment. On August 2, 1947, he defected by crossing from the Soviet sector to the British sector of Berlin, and from there he left for England.

In memoirs published in 1953, Foote confirmed some of Ruth Werner's statements about La Taupiniere, but certain differences are worth noting. Werner, who was operating under the alias of "Sonia," was in fact named Maria Schultz. Her husband, who is not named in her memoirs, was Alfred Schultz, who worked for the intelligence service of the Soviet Army in Poland

and the Far East, and who was in the Far East at the time. Hermann was actually Franz Ahlmann, who had been a German Communist for many years and who operated at the time of La Taupiniere under the cover name "Alex." The younger English-man, who supposedly used the name "Len" in Ruth Werner's memoirs, was really named Bill Philips and operated under the name "Jack."

In contrast to Ruth Werner's account, Foote maintains that Ruth Werner (or Maria Schultz) had already gathered a large number of people whom she could trust in Germany and was planning not only a major act of sabotage but even the assas-sination of Hitler—facts that Werner oddly doesn't mention. According to Foote, the Hitler-Stalin pact also affected Sonia more than she let on in her memoirs. Foote recalled that "the German-Russian Pact hit us like a thunderbolt out of a clear sky." He described the effect on Sonia as follows:

The first and only reaction to the Pact that we had from Moscow was a day later, when Sonia received a message to pull all the agents she could out of Germany and break all contact with any remaining resident agents. This was my first experience of Russian *Realpolitik*, and it came as something of a shock. Its effect on Sonia, who was an old Guard Com-munist who had for the past eight years regarded Fascism as the major world menace, was of course shattering. As a good Party member she had had Party discipline drilled into her until it was second nature for her to obey the whims of a Party directive, but she always regarded the main Party line as being firmly and steadfastly directed against Fascism. At one blow all this was changed, and she, as a good Party member, had now to regard the Nazis as her friends and the democracies as her potential foes. Such a *bouleversement* of all her pre-conceived ideas was really too much for her. Sonia, too, paid lip-service to her orders and obediently disbanded the orga-nization that she had been at such pains to build up; but I think that from that time onwards her heart was not in the work. She continued to obey such orders as she received and carried out operations to the best of her ability, but at the first opportunity she pulled out and returned to England. In a way she was lucky to have received her disillusionment early in the war. She had worked for many years for what she thought was a righteous cause, and she was spared the final discovery that the cause for which she had been working was not an idealistic crusade, but merely power politics in their crudest form.[58]

Foote reported that the entire clandestine operation was discontinued, as was the Red Orchestra in Brussels. Although "Sonia was wrestling with her political conscience," as he recalled in his memoirs, he had the difficult task of recalling the operatives from Germany.

George Charney: The Pact Left Weakness and Confusion Among American Communists

Outside of Europe, the pact had a particularly strong impact on American Communists, their sympathizers, and on many anti-Fascists in the United States. This is seen clearly in the memoirs of George Charney, who was thirty-four years old in 1939 and the organizational secretary of the CP USA for New England.

Influenced by Hitler's accession to power, Charney joined the CP USA in 1933. His views were strengthened by the anti-Fascist struggle during the period of the Popular Front: "The experience of the International Brigade in Spain, the offer of the Soviet Union to aid Czechoslovakia, the eloquent role of Litvinov at the League of Nations, the fervent pleas for anti-fascist unity, the readiness to implement it with military pacts, all combined to bolster my faith in the policies of the Communist movement and the Soviet government."

Charney's disillusionment was all the greater when the pact was announced:

> The signing of the Nazi-Soviet pact in August, 1939 thus came as a complete shock. . . . The shock was due in large part to the fact that we had become totally committed to the anti-Fascist struggle. The agony of Spain, events in Germany, the frightful anticipation of the world war, all of these had filled us with an implacable hatred of Hitlerism. The pact left us limp and confused. . . . Part of the shock was transmitted from the outside —from allies and friends, from the big Jewish community in New York, from my parents. And yet, such was our attachment to the party that we listened and accepted the explanations.

However, it was not easy to defend the party's new policy. Charney was to speak before party members and sympathizers in the Lower East Side of Manhattan. He recalled that the audience was "in an ugly mood. They listened in pain, however, as I retraced the appeasement history. . . . Yet I could establish no bond with the people, for it was only a part of the story, and I could feel the ache of uncertainty that continued for years to torment me and many of the comrades."

American Communists were especially devastated, in Charney's opinion, by Molotov's statement that "ideology was a matter of taste." He recalled that his friends in the party tried to ignore and forget this event, which was "as though we instinctively feared to analyze its implications. And yet, in spite of these shattering experiences, our faith held. The Soviet Union could not be wrong. It was still the socialist fatherland, the only force that could save the world from catastrophe. We managed to submerge our doubts."

In his memoirs, published in 1968, George Charney not only recorded his reaction to the pact but also addressed another important issue—namely, the thesis that, despite all its negative aspects, the pact was justified because it permitted the Soviet Union to stay out of the war and gain time for the final battle with Fascism:

> The Nazi-Soviet pact? In the war years it was forgotten; in reviewing this span of history it cannot be forgotten. The huge losses of manpower, civilian population, and resources suffered by the Soviet Union in the surprise attack makes a shambles of the old apologetic argument that it gave time for preparation. What preparation? Even a week prior to June 22, *Pravda* published a strong statement denouncing rumors of disagreements with Germany. It is still difficult to measure the moral setback suffered by the Communist movement in the West as a result of the pact. Perhaps some day a comprehensive critique will be made of this period by Soviet historians.[59]

One can safely imagine that there are many Soviet historians who would be all too prepared to subject this period to a "comprehensive critique." However, this was strictly forbidden before Mikhail Gorbachev was appointed General Secretary of the CPSU on March 11, 1985. The Hitler-Stalin pact itself, the developments that led to it, and the consequences could not be studied in the USSR until 1987. Not only the text of the Secret Protocol but even every reference to it was strictly forbidden until 1987–1988. Only now, since the Hitler-Stalin pact is openly discussed in Lithuania, Latvia, and Estonia, is it possible that this ban will be lifted. Only then will Soviet writing on the Second World War succeed in overcoming inner contradictions and partial truths.

Peggy Dennis in New York:
"Say It Isn't True!"

Peggy Dennis joined the CP USA as a young woman in 1925 in California. She was a party member for fifty-one years until she resigned in 1976. She traveled to Moscow for the first time in 1931. Her husband, Eugene Dennis, who later became the Secretary General of the CP USA, was active in the Far Eastern department of the Comintern. In the mid-1930s, both returned to the United States; they learned about the Hitler-Stalin pact in their New York apartment on 171st Street: "In utter shock I wailed and pleaded: Say it isn't true!" Her husband Gene tried to calm her and himself. "He stalked into the bedroom and at the desk thumbed through the large pile of manila folders which contained the newspaper clippings I worked on daily." Gene showed her Stalin's statement at the 18th Party Congress in March 1939. He recalled that the United States had recognized Franco's Fascist government at the beginning of April, and the difficulties encountered in the negotiations between the Western allies and the Soviet Union in the summer of 1939.

"All right, but this doesn't mean that overnight Fascism is acceptable," said Peggy Dennis. "No one says it does," replied her husband. "The Soviet Union has outwitted the bourgeois democracies in their attempts to get Germany and the Soviet Union to fight each other while they stand by, then pick up the pieces. That's all. Nothing else has changed."

In fact, however, Eugene Dennis was deeply shocked. Peggy Dennis recalled: "I saw little of Gene. He was in continual sessions downtown. He came home tense, preoccupied, silent, refusing to be drawn into discussion. He appeared deeply troubled."

In the meantime, Molotov's statement from the end of October had become known to the effect "that Hitler Fascism was 'just another ideology'; that 'one may accept or reject.' " With that, the problems and contradictions increased dramatically, and Peggy Dennis was truly dismayed: "I could understand the pragmatic, tactical character of the pact, but this reversal of analysis of Fascism and rejection of the years-long commitment to fight Fascism which dominated our international movement was reprehensible. . . . I demanded plausible answers, but Gene did not respond. He was in conflict. It was inconceivable to him that there could be a dichotomy between any Communist party and the Soviet Union."

But that was in fact what was at stake: the dependency of the CP USA on Soviet foreign political interests. Peggy Dennis summed up the situation in the following words: "So it was not the German-Soviet Pact that destroyed the anti-Fascist alignments and our relations with them. . . . It was the inability or unwillingness of the American party leadership, including Gene, to analyze the American scene independently from Moscow."[60]

Klaus Mehnert: The Reaction of Leftist American Students in Hawaii

Klaus Mehnert, the well-known German author and Soviet expert, learned about the Hitler-Stalin pact as a thirty-three-year-old professor of political science at the University of Hawaii. Mehnert, who was born in Moscow in 1906, grew up in Stuttgart. He began studying the Soviet Union in his youth: He visited the USSR in the Summer of 1932 and published a book entitled *Youth in Soviet Russia*. From 1934 until 1936, he was again in Moscow as a newspaper correspondent. Thereafter, he was a guest professor at the University of California at Berkeley and in 1937 became a professor of political science and contemporary history at the University of Hawaii in Honolulu. Mehnert recalled:

> Hitler's pact with Stalin was a shock for the left-leaning American intellectuals. They were not surprised about Hitler's behavior, since they thought him capable of any evil. They were, however, embittered by Stalin. For years they had defended Stalin against his critics with the argument that he opposed Hitler—and now he had made common cause with Hitler himself![61]

John Gates, CP USA: Deeply Hurt and Left to His Own Devices

John Gates also described the reaction of American Communists to the pact and the urgent need for a policy independent of Moscow's. Gates, who was born in New York in 1913, became acquainted with socialist ideas during his school years. His father lost his small shop during the Great Depression, and young John had to work after school and during the summer to help the family make ends meet. In March 1931, Gates joined the Young Communist League and was also active in the movement for the unemployed. He was a member of the CP USA from the ages of seventeen to forty-four, or from 1931 to 1958. At the end of 1936, he volunteered for the Lincoln Brigade to fight in the Spanish Civil War.

John Gates heard about the Hitler-Stalin pact after he returned to the United States; he recalled that it "came like a thunderclap. . . . Leaders and rank-and-file members were thrown into utter confusion. The impossible had happened. We looked hopefully for an escape clause in the treaty, but the official text provided none. For several days there was no clarification from

Moscow and we American Communists were left painfully on our own. It would have been better if we had remained on our own."

"A national conference of the Communist Party took place," Gates recalled, "amid pathetic consternation." Eugene Dennis, who was then the party's legislative secretary, called "for a fight on two fronts: against the Fascist enemy and against the appeasing democratic governments which could not be relied on to fight Fascism. This attitude," which Gates found reasonable given the situation, "did not last long." This political about-face severely damaged the CP USA:

> The complete turnabout cost us heavily. It lent credence to the charge that the policy of the anti-Fascist people's front was a Trojan horse maneuver, a tactic toward the end of securing complete power for ourselves, that our anti-Fascism was not sincere. Not only reactionaries but the entire democratic current denounced us. New epithets were coined at our expense: "red fascists" and "Communazis." There was a certain poetic justice in this since we had once called the Socialists "social-fascists." The truth was that regardless of Socialist or Communist mistakes, neither of them were ever any kind of Fascist. The unity we had helped to create, the alliances we had established with important forces in American life, were shattered overnight.

Many important people in the labor movement rejected any further cooperation with the Communists as a result of this development. The same was true of the National Negro Congress and the American Student Union. "Prominent intellectuals, like Granville Hicks, left the party. Even though our loss of members was far less severe, our loss of influence was important."[62]

Leon Trostky's Comments in Mexico

Leon Trotsky, Lenin's closest comrade-in-arms during the October Revolution of 1917 and the founder and leader of the Red Army during the Russian Civil War, was in Coyoacan in Mexico at the time of the Hitler-Stalin pact.

Trotsky was deported from the Soviet Union in 1928; he first went to Turkey, where he lived on the island of Prinkipo for four years. From 1933 until the summer of 1935, Trotsky lived in France, first in St. Palais near Royan on the Atlantic coast and later in Barbizon near Paris. Reactionary and Stalinist newspapers competed in "witch hunts" against Trotsky. He assumed the identity of an honorary Rumanian professor named Louis Level Leon and lived in hiding in a number of towns in France, in constant contact with the Trotskyite groups in different countries. At the same time, he worked on a biography of Lenin.

However, he was also unwelcome in France. After a long delay, the Social Democratic government of Norway granted him asylum. Trotsky arrived in Norway on June 15, 1935, and lived for a time in the home of the socialist publisher Knudsen in Vexhall near Hönefoss. Soon after his arrival, Trotsky was visited by the Social Democratic Minister of Justice, Trygve Lie, who was later Secretary General of the United Nations.

In Norway, Trotsky continued working on his biography of Lenin and began writing his most important book, *The Revolution Betrayed*. But even in Norway, he lived in constant danger: On the night of August 6, 1939, Norwegian Fascists who were supporters of Quisling forced their way into Trotsky's house and tried to steal some of his papers. Moreover, the Soviet Embassy demanded more and more forcibly that Trotsky be expelled from Norway, claiming that his continued presence would cause a rupture in Soviet-Norwegian relations. As a result of this pressure, the Norwegian government increased its control of Trotsky.

At the beginning of September 1936, Trotsky was interned in Sundby, 30 kilometers north of Oslo. He and his wife Natalja were watched by twenty policemen day and night. No one except for Trotsky's Norwegian lawyer could visit him. He had to obtain special permission to receive a newspaper, and his correspondence was read by a censor.

As a result, Trotsky was pleased when his friends, especially the Mexican painter Diego Rivera, cofounder of the CP Mexico, tried to obtain asylum for him in Mexico. On December 13, 1936, he was informed that the Mexican President Cardenas had granted Trotsky a residence permit. On December 19, Trotsky and his wife Natalja left Norway under police escort on the oil tanker "Ruth"; there were no other passengers. During the voyage, Trotsky analyzed the Moscow show trials against Zinoviev and Kamenev, which took place in August of 1936, and worked on his book *Stalin's Crimes*.

Trotsky and Natalja were concerned about the fate that awaited them in Mexico, but this time their fears were unfounded. They arrived in Mexico on January 9, 1937:

> In the hot, tropical morning, our tanker entered the harbor of Tampico. We were still in ignorance of what was awaiting us. . . . But everything had been safely arranged. Shortly after the tanker halted, a government cutter approached carrying representatives of the local federal authorities, Mexican and foreign journalists, and, most important of all, true and reliable friends. . . . After four months of imprisonment and isolation, this meeting with friends was especially cordial. The Norwegian policeman, who finally handed us our passports and revolvers, looked on with embarrassment at the courteous behavior of the Mexican police chief. . . . Torn free from the atmosphere of disgusting arbitrariness and enervating uncertainty, we encountered hospitality and attentiveness at every step.[63]

On January 11, Leon and Natalja Trotsky arrived in Coyoacan, a suburb of Mexico City, where they lived in the house of Diego Rivera. It was a roomy, bright blue house, decorated with Rivera's frescoes, and full of flowers and Mexican and Indian art objects. Trotsky recalled that an orange tree grew in the middle of the courtyard.

In the afternoon of January 11, Trotsky was visited by his friends Otto and Alice Rühle. Alice Rühle recorded this meeting in her diary, which was first published in 1979: "We sat down with him on the primitive leather chairs made by the Mexican Indios in the villages. . . . Trotsky was natural, gay, lively and quite youthful." He spoke to them in German, but when Diego Rivera entered switched to French; Alice Rühle noted that he spoke both languages almost flawlessly.

Trotsky reported on his trip on the small Norwegian ship that had brought him to Mexico, on the fact that he was closely guarded, that he was forbidden to listen to the radio, and that no one had told him where they would land. Then he reported on his sojourn in Scandinavia: "Trotsky spoke with irony and bitterness about Norway, which, under pressure from Russia, had first imprisoned and then deported him. He had told the Norwegian Minister of Justice, a Social Democrat: 'I will be avenged on you for this. Think of me when you are in exile.' "[64]

Trotsky's prophecy was true: Barely four years later, in April of 1940, the members of the Norwegian government, including the Minister of Justice, Trygve Lie, had to leave their country and spend several years as emigrés in London.

Until March 1939, Trotsky lived in the house of Diego Rivera. Rivera had been appointed to the Central Committee of the Mexican party in 1922, but had left the party at the end of the 1920s in protest over Stalin's suppression of the Trotskyites. Here in Coyoacan, at the end of 1937, Trotsky witnessed the second major show trial against Lenin's closest comrades-in-arms.

During this show trial, Trotsky was himself accused of having concluded a secret agreement with Hitler and the Emperor of Japan, the goal of which was the military defeat of the Soviet Union and the cession of the Ukraine to the Third Reich. Natalja Trotsky recalled: "With pencil in hand Lev Davidovich, over-tense and overworked, often in fever, yet tireless, lists the forgeries which have grown so numerous that it becomes impossible to refute them."[65]

Even in Mexico, Trotsky was not spared hostile attacks. The Mexican trade union federation was a Stalinist stronghold at the time, and the head of the federation, Lombardo Toledano, and the CP Mexico protested angrily because Trotsky had been given asylum in Mexico. They vowed not to rest until this "leader of the advance guard of counter-revolution" was expelled from the country. The threats became more open; police had to be posted in front of the Riveras' house while inside the house Trotskyites kept watch. It was here that Trotsky finished *Stalin's Crimes*, while maintaining lively contact with the outer world. He was visited by political emigrés from Europe and naturally by Trotskyites from many different countries.

Trotsky was among the few people who foresaw the Hitler-Stalin pact and who said so in print. After the treaty of Munich in the autumn of 1938, which meant, in effect, the surrender of Czechoslovakia, Trotsky prophesied: "The collapse of Czechoslovakia is the collapse of Stalin's international policy of the last five years. . . . We may now expect with certainty Soviet diplomacy to attempt *rapprochement* with Hitler at the cost of new retreats and capitulations."[66]

A few months later, in the spring of 1939, Trotsky left Diego Rivera's home and rented a house in the Avenida Viena outside of Coyoacan, where the street was empty, rocky, and dusty. Trotsky's wife Natalja recalled:

> We had rented a large, dilapidated house in Coyoacan, which had been restored very simply and which was surrounded by a fair-sized garden whose ancient trees were alive with bird-song every morning. The place was very isolated; on one side there was a wide stream, which was dry most of the time, and on the other a dusty road with some Mexican adobe hovels. We had a wall built round the grounds. Any visitor had to pass through a solid iron gate which a young comrade would only open if he had received explicit instructions and after he had examined the visitor through a spy-hole. Outside, the police had built a brick *casita* with a loophole, thirty paces from our gate. From inside it they watched over our safety. [67]

Trotsky concentrated on his work: correspondence, articles, books, notes for projected works. He signed a contract with the Harper publishing house to write a biography of Stalin; this book continuously occupied him. Natalja recorded that Trotsky would have much preferred to write another book of which he had dreamed for a long time, on the friendship and collaboration between Marx and Engels, on their common discoveries, and on their indestructable attachment to one another. With a certain sadness Natalja remarked that "the publishers and the public were much more interested in the fearsome tyrant." [68] In the midst of work on the biography of Stalin (which he was never to finish since he was murdered by a Stalinist agent on August 20, 1940), Trotsky learned of the Hitler-Stalin pact. In his first commentary, Trotsky emphasized the effects of the pact on the Communist International: "The Comintern, (the) most important instrument of the Kremlin for influencing public opinion in other countries, is in reality the first victim of the German-Soviet pact.

The fate of Poland has not yet been decided. But the Comintern is already a corpse."[69]

A few days later, but still before Soviet troops had invaded Poland, Trotsky pointed to the connection between the pact and the fate of Poland: "One thing is clear: the German-Soviet agreement facilitated the defeat of Poland."[70] When Soviet troops finally invaded Poland on September 17, 1939, thereby completing the partition of Poland between Hitler and Stalin, Trotsky prophesied: "Poland will resurrect, the Comintern never."[71]

In his most important commentary on the Hitler-Stalin pact, Trotsky pointed out that the agreement was not the result of a sudden decision by the Kremlin but of a long development, and that the show trials of 1936–1938 against Lenin's former comrades-in-arms served to pave the way for the pact with Nazi Germany:

> Today it is clear that in the very same years in which the Comintern was bringing to a head its clamorous campaign for an alliance of the democracies against Fascism, the Kremlin was preparing a military understanding with Hitler against the so-called democracies. Even complete idiots will have to understand now that the Moscow trials, with the aid of which the Bolshevik Old Guard was destroyed under the accusation of collaboration with the Nazis, were nothing but camouflage for the Stalinist alliance with Hitler. The secret is out.[72]

Trotsky—The Pact of 1939 and Brest-Litovsk, 1918

Leon Trotsky was probably the only contemporary of the Hitler-Stalin pact who dealt with an argument that was discussed by

reflective party members in many countries as a possible justification of the pact, namely that the Hitler-Stalin pact of 1939
was similar to Lenin's peace treaty of Brest-Litovsk in 1918.

The Treaty of Brest-Litovsk was well known to Communists
in 1939. The Bolsheviks, who came to power in November of
1917, had first offered peace to all the peoples of the world.
However, England, France, and other countries of the Entente
had not accepted the proposals of the Soviet government. At the
same time, the troops of the German Kaiser pressed forward into
Soviet Russia at great speed. The Bolsheviks could not oppose
them, since the tsarist army had collapsed and the Red Army
was only being formed. Since Soviet Russia was weak it had no
other alternative but to compromise with the German Empire,
ceding it large portions of its territory in exchange for peace.

In view of the experience of Brest-Litovsk, some Communists
drew the following conclusion: In 1918, Lenin made a compromise to obtain peace for Soviet Russia; the same was true in
1939, when the Soviet Union was again in danger of being
attacked by German imperialism. As in 1918, some argued, the
pact of August 1939 was a distasteful but necessary compromise.
It was exactly this argument, the reader may recall, which was
forwarded by Jiri Pelikan's older brother. Trotsky commented
on this attempt to justify the pact as follows:

> There are people who dare to compare the Stalin-Hitler
> alliance with the treaty of Brest-Litovsk. What a mockery!
> The Brest-Litovsk negotiations were carried out openly before
> all humanity. The Soviet revolution, at the end of 1917 and
> beginning of 1918, didn't have even a single batallion capable
> of carrying on the fight. Hohenzollern Germany attacked Rus-
> sia, taking Soviet provinces and military supplies. The young
> government had no other physical possibility than to sign the
> peace treaty. This peace was openly defined by us as a ca-
> pitulation of a disarmed revolution before a powerful en-

emy. . . . The present Stalin-Hitler pact was concluded despite the existence of an army of several millions, and the immediate task of the pact was to facilitate Hitler's smashing of Poland and its division between Berlin and Moscow. Where is the analogy?[73]

In comparing the Treaty of Brest-Litovsk of 1918 with the Hitler-Stalin pact of 1939, Trotsky could have mentioned Lenin's famous distinction between permissible and necessary compromises on the one hand and categorically impermissible compromises on the other. In the spring of 1920, Lenin explained the compromise of Brest-Litovsk with his parable of armed bandits:

> Imagine that your automobile is held up by armed bandits. You hand them over your money, passport, revolver and automobile. You are spared the pleasant company of the bandits. That is unquestionably a compromise. *"Do ut des"* ("I give" you money, firearms, automobile, "so that you give" me the opportunity to depart in peace). But it would be difficult to find a sane man who would declare such a compromise to be "inadmissible on principle," or who would proclaim the compromiser an accomplice of the bandits (even though the bandits might use the automobile and the firearms for further robberies). Our compromise with the bandits of German imperialism was a compromise of such a kind.

On the other hand, Lenin continued, there were also compromises in which the victim didn't ransom his freedom but in which a person supported the bandits in order to share the booty with them. Such a person is the bandits' accomplice. Lenin called this "treachery," an example of

> the worst kind of opportunism, treachery and betrayal. . . . There are compromises and compromises. One must be able

to analyse the situation and the concrete conditions of each compromise, or of each variety of compromise. One must learn to distinguish between a man who gave the bandits money and firearms in order to lessen the evil committed by them and to facilitate the task of getting them captured and shot, and a man who gives bandits money and firearms in order to share in the loot.[74]

This was exactly the distinction between the Treaty of Brest-Litovsk in 1918 and the Hitler-Stalin pact of 1939. In 1918, Soviet Russia had no alternative but to make a compromise, ceding certain parts of its territory in order to purchase peace. Soviet Russia was, to remain with Lenin's analogy, the victim who gave the bandits his car, money, and passport in order to save his life. The Hitler-Stalin pact, however, was just the opposite: This was a treaty whose most important aspects were secret, whose primary purpose was the delineation of spheres of influence, the joint occupation of a third nation—Poland— and the joint suppression of its people. In 1939, the Soviet Union was, to use Lenin's analogy, not the victim who was ransoming himself but a person who was voluntarily acting as the bandits' accomplice, who reached an agreement with them in order to "participate in sharing the booty."[75]

4

THE PACT AND CHANGES OF
ATTITUDES: FIVE EXAMPLES

Among the many contemporaries of the pact discussed so far, there remains an especially important category: those for whom the Hitler-Stalin pact was such a decisive turning point that they broke with Stalinism and the world communist movement directed from Moscow. In Soviet historiography—and this is also true for the German Democratic Republic and several other Eastern European countries—such people have been termed "renegades," which, parenthetically, was a term also used by the Catholic church in the Middle Ages for Christians who converted to Islam. Sometimes these renegades are also called "enemies"; after his conversation with the critical writer Gustav Regler, Alexander Abusch explained "that yesterday's friends could become today's enemies."[1]

In some cases, more lofty explanations were given for those who broke with communism—for example, that those in question did not possess sufficient steadfastness in a period of increasing international class struggle because of their petit bourgeois tendencies. In any event, a break with communism was, as Hans Werner Richter described, a long, painful and often distressing process, the loss of an ideal to which one had clung, the abandonment of a belief that resembled faith in salvation.[2]

The following are examples of people who, after years of communist activity, inspired especially by the anti-Fascist struggle during the period of the Popular Front, felt their first doubts in connection with the mass arrests and the show trials in the Soviet Union in the mid-1930s. They still trusted Moscow because the Soviet Union seemed to be the standard-bearer of anti-Fascism, however, the Hitler-Stalin pact broke this last bond of loyalty and made it impossible for them to remain any longer in the communist movement.

Granville Hicks: The Pact and His Resignation from the CP USA

John Gates mentioned the most important of the prominent intellectuals who left the CP USA as a result of the Hitler-Stalin pact—Granville Hicks, who did much for the CP USA during the Popular Front and who brought the party far more influence and prestige than it had had until then. Granville Hicks was born to a middle-class family in New England. After receiving his B.A. from Harvard College in 1923, he attended the Harvard Divinity School, and from 1928 to 1929, the English Department of the Graduate School. At Harvard, Hicks was among the students who were interested in politics, but he only became politically active in 1927, when, as a professor at Smith College, he participated in the protests against the conviction of Sacco and Vanzetti.

The misery of the Great Depression convinced him that only a total transformation of the entire economic system could free the United States from the scourge of unemployment. Hicks became acquainted with socialists and with Communists; at first, he was inclined to favor the former but then gradually moved closer to the latter, because they were supported by Marxist theory and could point to the Soviet Union as an example of the implementation of this theory.

In the autumn of 1932, Hicks and other prominent American intellectuals signed a widely noted appeal to support the Communist candidate in the presidential election. Hicks and his friends began to read Marx, Engels, and Lenin; they were impressed by the criticism of capitalism and especially by the laws of historical development—which they viewed as the "key to history"—which would lead to the formation of a classless society. From the beginning of 1934, Hicks was increasingly active in Communist-inspired organizations. He became the editor of the Communist weekly *New Masses*, but still did not join the party.

The turning point for Hicks was the 7th World Congress of the Communist International in the summer of 1935 and the new Popular Front policy. Up until then, Hicks had been skeptical of the left sectarian tactic of the Communist party, which meant that the American Communists refused to cooperate with other progressive forces, especially with the socialists. The Popular Front policy changed all that. Hicks, deeply impressed by Georgij Dimitroff's speech at the 7th World Congress and by the new policies of the United Front and Popular Front, joined the CP USA. He recalled that party propaganda ceased to focus on the USSR and concentrated on American problems. The party's influence grew rapidly: The membership in the CP USA increased from 12,000 in 1929 to almost 100,000 in the Popular Front period. Hicks joined the party because he was a convinced Marxist, because he strove to build a socialist society, and, above all, because he saw the CP USA as the primary bulwark against Fascism. When he joined the party he was convinced that he was participating in a decisive historical process—he was a comrade-in-arms in an active political force. At a time when others only posed questions and criticized, the CP USA seemed to be a party of action. As a party member, Hicks showed the dangers of Fascism and supported the victims of Nazi tyranny. He participated in campaigns in support of Spain and was active in the trade union movement, which experienced an impressive revival at the time. At the same time, he published two successful books: a biography of the American Communist John Reed (*John Reed: Biography of a Communist by a Communist*, 1936) and 1937's *I Like America*, in which he combined his love of the American people with a discussion of the injustice and evil in the country.

However, several things troubled Hicks during this period: the mass arrests and the show trials in the Soviet Union, the accusations of treason against men who shortly before had been model fighters for revolution to American Communists. Nevertheless, Hicks suppressed these doubts, since he considered the Soviet Union to be the main opponent of Fascism; he had, he wrote, no right to allow his personal doubts to influence his views of the great struggle against Fascism.

Then came the Hitler-Stalin pact: "I remember very well the moment at which we got the news of the Soviet-Nazi nonaggression pact. For some reason we had not listened to the late news the night before, and so I had been given a good night's sleep that I wasn't, so to speak, entitled to. Then at breakfast, on a beautiful summer morning, we heard the report. When I was able to speak, I said, 'That knocks the bottom out of everything.' "

Hicks described his first reaction to the pact in the following words: "The behavior of the American Comunists in August 1939, when Russia signed the nonaggression pact with Germany, opened my eyes on the first score. In this moment of crisis the leaders of the party could not conceal the fact that their primary function was to defend Russia, no matter what it did. They even made it clear that they had to wait for Russia to tell them in what terms the defense was to be made—had to wait for the Kremlin to give them the new line. This was not the kind of party I thought I had belonged to, and I got out."

Hicks justified his resignation from the party as follows: "When I quit the party, it was on the grounds that the party had acted contrary to all its professed principles and had revealed its complete subservience to Russia." When Hicks discussed the matter with other comrades, they continuously repeated the argument that was so widespread at that time—namely, that the Soviet Union had no other choice than to conclude a pact with Hitler because the Western powers—especially Chamberlain during the meeting in Munich in September 1938—had betrayed the common alliance against Fascism. Hicks was not impressed by these arguments and forwarded an important objection, which could not be easily dismissed:

> If Chamberlain's Munich was a betrayal, wasn't Stalin's Munich-in-reverse equally a betrayal? It was said, of course, that Stalin had no choice: Munich had demonstrated that he must betray or be betrayed. But could not the same thing be said in defense of Chamberlain? Might he not have been convinced that if he had got himself embroiled with Hitler over Czechoslovakia, Stalin would have left England and France holding the bag? And didn't the events of 1939 suggest that Chamberlain's fears were justified, for hadn't Stalin made a deal with Hitler as soon as France and England were firmly committed to the defense of Poland?

Granville Hicks noted that those comrades who stepped forward advocated cold *realpolitik* at the expense of all moral considerations: "Russia's actions, they asserted, had to be judged in terms of *realpolitik*; moral principles were strictly irrelevant. But it was on moral grounds that I and many others had been defending the Soviet Union." Hicks summed up the effect of the pact as follows: "One thing was clear: the prestige Communism had briefly enjoyed among the intellectuals was dead."[3]

Arthur Koestler's Final Break

The well-known writer Arthur Koestler's break with Stalinist communism occurred in two phases: At the beginning of 1938, he announced in a letter that he was officially leaving the party but did not mention the Soviet Union, which he still believed to be a bulwark of anti-Fascism. Koestler's final break took place after the Hitler-Stalin pact. His life is so well known, especially owing to his extensive memoirs, that it will suffice here to mention only the most important events in Koestler's life before focusing on the last months before the Hitler-Stalin pact and his reaction to it.

Arthur Koestler was born in Budapest in 1905 and witnessed the beginnings of the Hungarian Soviet Republic as a fourteen-year-old boy. He moved to Vienna, where he studied the natural sciences, and even worked on a kibbutz in Palestine. From 1925 until 1930, he worked as a foreign correspondent for the newspapers of the Ullstein publishing house—first in the Middle East and then in Paris. In 1930, he moved to Berlin, arriving on September 14, the day the Nazis achieved their breakthrough in the elections to the Reichstag. At that time, Koestler was the science editor of the *Vossische Zeitung*, published by Ullstein, and the scientific advisor for the other Ullstein publications. He was also active for the newspaper *BZ am Mittag*. Koestler recalled writing about electrons, chromosomes, rockets, Neanderthal men, and spiral nebula. At the same time, he could not escape the increasing pressure of political events: the worldwide depression, the rapid increase in the number of unemployed, and the Nazi menace were decisive events for him. "With one-third of its wage earners unemployed, Germany lived in a state of latent civil war, and if one wasn't prepared to be swept along as a passive victim by the approaching hurricane it became imperative to take sides," Koestler recalled. "The Socialists pursued a policy of opportunist compromise. Even by a process of pure elimination, the Communists, with the mighty Soviet Union behind them, seemed the only force capable of resisting the onrush of the primitive horde with its swastika totem."[4]

However, it was not only the circumstances in which he found himself that turned him to communism, but his study of the works of Marx, Engels, and Lenin, which, as he wrote, "shook me like a mental explosion." From now on, there seemed to be a clear answer to every question; doubts and conflicts belonged to the distant past when one lived in shameful ignorance in the drab world of the uninitiated.

On December 31, 1931, Koestler joined the Communist party of Germany; he explained his act in a letter to the Central Committee and soon received a reply, which requested him to come to an exchange of views. His interlocutor from the party was Ernst Schneller, a member of the Central Committee and director of the Department of Agitation and Propaganda (Agit-prop). Koestler soon learned that Schneller was also in one of the party's secret organizations. Schneller advised him not to be openly active in one of the party's organizations, but to continue as a secret member: "You will not be assigned to a cell and will be known in the Party under a different name," Schneller explained. Koestler chose the cover name Ivan Steinberg; from now on there were regular "chats"—meetings at which Arthur Koestler, alias Ivan Steinberg, dictated whatever information he heard at the Ullstein publishing house.

Several months later his intelligence activity at Ullstein was discovered, and his contacts with the party apparatus were broken off. Koestler became what he had originally wanted to be: a "real" party member in a party "cell," as the grass-roots organization of the CP Germany was called.

However, this was most certainly not a typical party cell: Arthur Koestler belonged to the cell of the artists' colony at the Laubenheimer Platz in Berlin, which was most unusual. The political director of the cell was Alfred Kantorowicz, the organizational director was the writer Max Schröder, and among the twenty members of the cell was Dr. Wilhelm Reich, the founder and director of the Institute for Sexual Politics. Koestler experienced the CP Germany's insane policy of refusing to forward a common candidate with the Social Democrats in the presidential elections of 1932 and of combatting the Social Democrats with the slogan "social Fascists." Koestler joined in this propaganda and attended cell meetings—which often ended in monotonous unanimity—but he also participated in frequent skirmishes with the Nazis.

In the late summer of 1932, several months before Hitler seized power, Koestler traveled to the Soviet Union on the invitation of the International Federation of Revolutionary Writers. He was commissioned to write an article entitled "A Man of the Middle Class Travels Through Soviet Russia," which was to describe how a middle-class reporter with anti-Soviet prejudices is gradually converted to communism as he sees the achievements of the construction of socialism and returns home as a party member. Koestler arrived in the Soviet Union in the middle of the harshest period of collectivization. He witnessed the devastation caused by the famine of 1932–33 in the Ukraine, the masses of tattered families who begged in the railway stations, the hunger and misery, the apathy of the people in the streets, the unbelievable living conditions, the starvation rations in the cooperatives. However, Koestler recorded that "My Party education had equipped my mind with such elaborate shock-absorbing buffers and elastic defenses that everything seen and heard became automatically transformed to fit the preconceived pattern."[5]

Hitler had already seized power when Koestler returned to Germany in the autumn of 1933, and so he joined his party friends in exile in Paris. The focus of the group and its most dynamic member was Willi Münzenberg, the head of the Agitation and Propaganda Department of the Comintern for Western Europe. Koestler characterized him as

> a short, stocky man of proletarian origin; a magnetic personality of immense driving power and a hard, seductive charm. Willi was the Red Eminence of the international anti-Fascist movement. . . . He produced International Committees, Congresses and Movements as a conjurer produces rabbits out of his hat: the "Committee to Aid the Victims of Fascism," the so-called "Committees for Vigilance and Democratic Control," international youth congresses, and more. Each of these covert Party organizations could proudly point to a list of highly respected people who were patrons or directors—among them some English duchesses, American columnists and French scholars, most of whom had never heard the name "Münzenberg" and who considered the Comintern a bogeyman invented by Goebbels.[6]

Koestler worked in the Institute for the Study of Fascism in Paris—one of the many organizations founded by Willi Münzenberg. He worked ten to twelve hours a day without a salary. His only privilege was the right to eat a big bowl of thick pea soup on the Rue Bouffon each noontime.

Koestler went to Spain during the Civil War and was taken prisoner when Malaga was captured by Franco's troops at the beginning of 1937. He spent four months in Franco's prisons in Malaga and Seville, most of it in solitary confinement in a sort of death cell, expecting his execution. To his surprise, he was set free in June 1937, when the British government intervened on his behalf. The dreadful experience in Franco's prisons at first strengthened his ties to the Communist party. Upon crossing the border at Gibraltar, Koestler sent a telegram to the party leadership saying, "cured of all stomach pains"; "stomach pains" was party slang for doubts that the party line was right. Koestler went to England where he wrote his famous book *A Spanish Testament*, which in short order became a selection of the well-known "Left Book Club" and was popular around the world.

Nevertheless, it was 1937, and almost ever day Koestler received news about the Great Purge in the Soviet Union with its mass arrests. His closest friends were among those arrested—especially Alex Weißberg, who told Koestler when the latter left the Soviet Union in 1933: "Whatever happens, hold high the banner of the Soviet Union." Now Alex Weißberg was a prisoner of the NKVD.

In the autumn of 1937, Koestler returned to Paris from England. On the first day after his arrival, two representatives of the party met him in a little cafe near the Place de la Bastille and subjected him to a formal interrogation about his actions while Franco's prisoner. One of the two party officials was Paul Merker; Koestler did not learn the identity of the second interrogator.

Such interrogations were, as a rule, not uncommon. A Communist released from prison always had to let the party's security members question him in detail in order to determine whether or not the former prisoner was still reliable. In Koestler's case, the procedure was more or less a harmless formality because Koestler had been freed as part of an international exchange of prisoners and had not had any illegal contacts in Spain that he could have betrayed. Nevertheless, the interrogation filled him with panic:

> I had a sudden, intense attack of anxiety, and I noticed how unsteady my hand was as I lifted the cup of cold *cafe au lait*. This was the Autumn of 1937; a few weeks earlier Marshal Tuchachevsky and eight top-ranking Generals of the Red Army had been shot after a secret trial; every day we heard of new arrests, accompanied by incredible and frightening accusations. The harmless interrogation of a moment ago carried a terrifying echo. It was impossible not to think how helpless one would be facing that taciturn, hard-eyed man, not at a Paris cafe table, but across the Prosecutor's desk in the G.P.U. building in Baku or in the Lubyanka. . . . The Terror was roaring across Russia, like a tidal wave drowning everybody on its way, and even a small, distant ripple of it made the cup tremble in one's hand in a Paris cafe.[7]

In March 1938, Koestler learned of the trial against the so-called anti-Soviet block, with Nikolai Bukharin as the main defendant. Koestler wrote that this trial surpassed all those which preceded it in absurdity and horror. A few days later, he was to deliver a lecture on Spain to the Association to Protect German Writers in the lecture hall of the Société des Industries Françaises at the Place St. Germain des Pres. The audience comprised 200 to 300 emigré intellectuals, most of whom were Communists. This was Koestler's first public appearance in Paris since he returned from Spain, and he felt that it would be his last as a party member. He had no intention of attacking the party so long as the war continued in Spain, and still less intention of criticizing the Soviet Union. On the other hand, he felt the need to clarify his position and not to remain the passive accomplice of his friends' executioners. Although he usually spoke extemporaneously, he wrote down the conclusion of his speech. It consisted of three carefully formulated sentences that were commonplaces for ordinary people but a mortal sin for Stalinists: "The first was: 'No movement, party or person can claim the privilege of infallibility.' The second was: 'Appeasing the enemy is as foolish as persecuting the friend who pursues your own aim by a different road.' The third was a quotation from Thomas Mann: 'A harmful truth is better than a useful lie.' "

When Koestler finished, the non-Communists in the audience applauded while the Communists remained demonstrably silent, most of them with arms crossed. He went home alone; as he waited for the train in the St. Germain des Pres subway station, some of his comrades who had attended the lecture descended the stairs into the station. They walked by him to the other end of the platform without looking at him or exchanging a word. This was a taste of the isolation he would experience in the months and years to come.

Several days later, he worked almost the entire night on his farewell letter to the CP Germany, the Comintern, and the Stalinist regime, but ended it with a declaration of loyalty to the Soviet Union. Despite all his criticism of the regime, of the cancer of bureaucracy, of the suppression and terror, he still confessed his faith in the unshakeable foundation of the workers' and peasants' state and in the nationalization of the means of production; he declared that "in spite of everything, the Soviet Union still represented our last and only hope on a planet in rapid decay."

Koestler definitively turned his back on communism only one year later. "I remained in that state of suspended animation until the day when the swastika was hoisted on Moscow Airport in honor of Ribbentrop's arrival and the Red Army band broke into the *Horst Wessel Lied*. That was the end; from then onward I no longer cared whether Hitler's allies called me a counter-revolutionary."[8]

Hans Werner Richter: The Party's Membership Books Were Burned

Hans Werner Richter is primarily known in Germany for his literary activity after World War II: as a cofounder of the magazine *Der Ruf*, the founder of and an active participant in the "Gruppe 47," and especially for his many books and literary awards. In contrast, it is not very well known that Richter was a member of the CP Germany from 1930 until the Hitler-Stalin pact in August of 1939 and was active for the party in the underground. This he recorded in a remarkable book entitled *Letters to a Young Socialist*, which is, in essence, a farewell to a utopian idea.

Richter was born in 1908 in Bansin on the island of Usedom, to parents who were fishermen. In the late 1920s, he worked as a clerk in a book shop in Berlin. He joined the CP Germany in 1930, largely for the following two reasons: "On the one hand there was the Soviet Union, about which we knew nothing specific, and which appeared radiant to us," Richter recalled, "while on the other there was the constant and unexpected advance of the National Socialists (Nazis) on which we didn't count since we believed that the course of history was on our side." John Reed's eyewitness account of the Russian Revolution, *Ten Days That Shook the World*, was one of the books that

influenced Richter the most. He read G. V. Plekhanov and Bukharin and obtained everything he could from the "leftist" publishing houses, including *30 Writers of Revolutionary Russia.*
Lenin and Trotsky became for Richter monumental figures of
world history, and the Soviet Union the ideal society, in which
there would be no class distinctions and no alienation of man.
And so he came to believe that the Russian comrades were the
avant-garde of the international revolution, called to lead and
be responsible for the German comrades, without realizing that
the circumstances in Germany in the early 1930s were utterly
different from those in Russia in 1917.

The other phenomenon, the advance of National Socialism,
surprised both him and other Communists in Germany, but he
was firmly convinced that it was an ephemeral phenomenon—
mere sound and fury, a last flickering of reaction, with no chance
of success.

Richter believed in the Marxist view that history developed
according to laws, from one prescribed period to another: from
feudalism to capitalism, from capitalism to socialism, and finally
to the victory of the proletariat. He described himself in 1930
as "a young functionary who believed that he not only possessed
truth—even absolute truth—but also possessed the great Marxist scalpel with which he could dissect everything and anything
and a divining-rod which would safely guide him out of the night
of the Republic into the sunlight of socialism."

To be sure, even then Hans Richter had a few doubts—
"political stomach aches" as the Communists called them.
Among these, the theory of "social Fascism," which stated that
social democracy was the main enemy, seemed false to him. He
also disapproved of the use of informants, of the atmosphere of
distrust, of suffocating all forms of democracy within the party,
and of transferring the methods of the Bolshevik party part and

parcel to the German CP. Despite these doubts, he continued to put up posters at night, participate in demonstrations, and found new local Communist organizations in villages in Pommerania. He continued to underestimate the danger of National Socialism—due to his fatal trust in "history," which left no room for doubt in the established victory of the proletariat. The Communist party was so weakened by internal struggles and the exclusion of members that it was destitute when Hitler seized power in January of 1933.

Richter was deeply shaken by the defeat of the CP Germany in January 1933. "Nothing moved, nothing happened, no strike, no general strike, no call to battle in the streets—nothing," Richter recalled. In his opinion, both parties of the left were responsible: The Social Democrats believed in legality—Hitler as provisional chancellor—while the Communists believed that it was only a brief, counterrevolutionary episode that would soon be to their advantage. Richter, who was then twenty-five years old, recalled: "The socialist and Communist youth, ready to take the fight to the streets, waited in vain for orders that never came, except for the instruction of the Communist Party to creep into the underground." Together with other youths, Richter waited in inner courtyards to "strike out," but they were only told to "wait" or "go home; we'll see what happens tomorrow." Nothing happened, nothing came. Richter recalled that "this was the first disillusionment for many of my contemporaries."

Richter was in Berlin when the witch hunt of Communists began upon Hitler's seizure of power and increased after the burning of the Reichstag: "This 'hunt' was at best the hunting of rabbits by assassins. There was no discussion, no defense, no struggle, only fear, fatalism, opportunism. The only solidarity was the solidarity in flight, not in battle." Night after night, one fled to the other seeking refuge, without direction, without knowing where and how they were to fight back. Many of Richter's friends were arrested; some escaped, while some leaders went with surprising speed abroad.

Those friends and comrades who hadn't emigrated or been arrested met in a lamentable little bookshop, which was also a sort of lending library. Hans Werner Richter hid anti-Fascist literature, as well as comrades who had gone underground and who moved from apartment to apartment. However, with the passage of each week and each month, fewer and fewer visitors came; one after the other disappeared.

At the beginning of November 1933, Richter went to Paris, where he met many friends living in wretched poverty. This was a continuation of the demoralization begun in Germany. Sometimes they talked in dreary rooms until dawn broke: What mistakes had they made? What had to be changed? How had the Communist party failed? They could find no convincing answers. The official emigré leadership of the CP Germany did not, it seemed to him, even register the defeat. There was not a word of self-criticism, which was long overdue, and some party officials even succeeded in calling the defeat a victory.

Richter wanted to fight the enemy where it counted—in his own country. And so he returned in April 1934, afraid of the terror and afraid of being discovered. Defeatism and resignation reached a high point in Germany at this time. The Nazi system had begun to take root and to penetrate everything and everyone. Richter maintained contact with young Marxists and other anti-Fascists. The desire for theoretical discussions had faded; what remained was the opposition to the Nazi system, with one goal—the elimination of Hitler. One's previous party affiliation no longer meant anything. Those who opposed Hitler, be they conservatives, Communists, Social Democrats, or Catholics, recognized each other by trivial gestures, facial expressions, and the like. They encountered one another everywhere—in factories, on the street, in shops. However, Hitler's increasing success in the realm of foreign policy did not help to strengthen the opposition and was difficult for the German anti-Fascists to bear. Only one hope remained: an embroilment abroad, which would be a stumbling block to Hitler's success and which would at last show him the limits of his power. This hope was pinned in part on the Western democracies, but the greatest hope was, and remained, the Soviet Union.

Hans Werner Richter and his friends applauded the outbreak of the Spanish Civil War: Now, they thought, the ideal of the Popular Front—the common struggle of all opponents of Fascism and genuine international solidarity—would become a reality. However, these hopes were overshadowed by the mass arrests in the Soviet Union and by the show trials in Moscow. One-half of the generals of the Red Army, led by Marshal Tukhachevsky, were cowardly traitors? Bukharin shot? The charges which the accused brought against themselves, the language—jackals, monsters, loathsome dogs, wolves in sheeps' clothing—all this from old Bolsheviks who had fought for half a century for the ideal of socialism?

Richter and his friends couldn't believe it. They were comforted by the realization that they were somewhat cut off from these events and poorly informed because they were largely dependent on the Nazi press, which was only propaganda. "We repressed what we didn't want to admit, because we had to repress it," Richter recalled. "Should we have destroyed our own, perhaps our only hope before our very eyes and the eyes of others? We couldn't do that and so we didn't." Despite some doubts, the Soviet Union remained the bulwark of opposition to Fascism, the only hope they had.

In August 1939, Richter was in Bansin, the Baltic seaside resort where he was born. He had left Berlin because of the danger of war and was working in his father's little gas station.

He wanted to be with his family and friends, who were almost all Social Democrats or Communists, while they waited to see what would happen. They foresaw the war and were convinced that Hitler would lose it, since he would be opposed by the Soviet Union, Poland, France, and England, with the United States behind them. In their opinion, such a war on two fronts could only last a few months. A war of endurance, lasting years, seemed impossible. Then came August 23, 1939, the day of the Hitler-Stalin pact:

It is August 23, 1939, the day on which all our hopes proved to be illusions, a day of utter humiliation and disappointment for me, yes of shame towards all those to whom I had, time and again, given hope with my arguments and persuaded to be patient. What were all the setbacks which we had experienced compared with this one day on which everything in which I had believed collapsed. No theory on the proper strategy against imperialism, no matter how marvellous it might be, could ever blot this day out of my life. That day cannot be hushed up, covered up with lies, rendered insignificant or, as one did after the war for reasons which are easily understood, made harmless. That day remained what it was: a day of unparalleled, traditional betrayal.

The consequences for the German socialists and for the international proletarian movement were devastating: it was pure and simple demoralization. Suddenly we were alone, abandoned, powerless. No one can measure the loss of moral strength to resist which occurred on this day alone. Hitler would have met his end much sooner if the Soviet Union had acted differently. Imagine what the day meant to us on which the flag with a Swastika was flown at the Moscow airport to honor Ribbentrop and therefore Hitler. . . . It was moral, political and psychological betrayal which not only caused the collapse of the Soviet myth, which reduced the resistance of the Communist Party to a mere phrase, which disavowed all of us, no matter where we were on the left, leaving us with a feeling of being handed over and sacrificed.

Richter recalled that his friends had said nothing, only shaken their heads in silence and disbelief, for they knew that Hitler would now declare war on Poland. "With the friendship and non-aggression pact with the Soviet Union in hand he could now risk anything, both at home and abroad."

The goal, the ideal of socialism, had become an illusion overnight, or at best a distant hope that perhaps could become reality several centuries later. The Soviet Union had thrown the ideals of the Popular Front, the common struggle against Fascism, overboard like unwanted baggage. "Many intellectuals," recalled Hans Werner Richter, "and also many workers and lower officials in Europe sent back their Party cards. We couldn't do that, but the following night I burned the Party records of an entire local organization which a friend had kept despite the fact that his safety was endangered. I burned them in the forest and then buried the ashes in order to be sure that they wouldn't be found. It was my last farewell to the Communist Party, to which there could be no return."⁹

Louis Fischer Found His Kronstadt

Granville Hicks was a party member from 1935 to 1939, Arthur Koestler from 1931 to 1939, and Hans Werner Richter from 1930 to 1939. Louis Fischer was never a party member but had lived, except for brief interruptions, in the Soviet Union from 1922 on and was, in retrospect, well-disposed toward the USSR. Scarcely any other foreigner had experienced such a long period of Soviet history so intensively as Fischer.

Louis Fischer grew up in Philadelphia and began working

as a free-lance journalist in Europe in December 1921. At this time, he was sympathetic to the Bolsheviks: "The Bolsheviks were for the international brotherhood of workers. They wanted to eliminate racial discrimination, abolish exploitation, inequality, the power of the rich, the privileges of kings and the passion for conquest." These goals also appealed to Louis Fischer: "For the first time a government dared to fulfill the dreams of the reformers, iconoclasts and protagonists of every age." The international character of the Bolshevik appeals was unprecedented at that time. Fischer was particularly impressed that the goal of the appeals was not only to change Russia but to abolish war, poverty, and suffering throughout the world. He traveled to Moscow for the first time in September 1922 and attended the 4th World Congress of the Comintern in November of that year. He met Lenin, Trotsky, and Zinoviev and at times acted more as a participant than as an observer and journalist.[10]

The Soviet Union was in the midst of the New Economic Policy (NEP) and was guided by relatively young and dynamic Bolshevik leaders—a fact that particularly impressed Fischer: In 1922, Lenin was fifty-two years old, Trotsky and Stalin forty-three, Zinoviev and Kamenev thirty-nine, Radek thirty-seven, and Bukharin only thirty-four. "The enthusiasm was infectious," Fischer recalled.

> Why should other governments and foreign diplomats and correspondents in Moscow obstruct or hide the efforts of a great nation to extricate itself from the mire? Since I too was born and raised in poverty I instinctively welcomed every effort to eliminate it. . . . The Revolution was a complete break with the past. Those were the most appealing aspects. . . . I marvelled at their courage. No one could doubt their earnestness. Internationalism stood at the top of the list of Communist virtues.

Fischer was critical of certain aspects, which he discussed with his Soviet friends in Moscow, but when he traveled in Europe and the United States he always defended the Soviet Union. However, from conversations in the Soviet Union he learned of the "Kronstadt blood bath" of March 1921, in which the uprising of revolutionary sailors of Kronstadt, supported by the local populace, was brutally suppressed by the Bolsheviks, who were already becoming bureaucratic. He talked with people for whom Kronstadt was the turning point, the cause of their break with Bolshevism. For Fischer, however, it took many years before he found his "Kronstadt." The Soviet promise fired his imagination during the 20s: "The Bolshevik capital was the future," he recalled. "Each new five year plan was presented as a difficult but necessary step towards attaining the new world. How could one complain about the shortage of potatoes when we were building socialism? Weren't we prepared to give up butter for Dneprostroj and Magnitogorsk, since they meant more hydroelectric power, more steel and ultimately more butter?" The industrial projects of the five-year plans, the factories and dams were the music of socialism for Fischer, the overture of the new social order. He felt close ties to the construction projects, which he frequently visited. The construction projects of the First Five Year Plan impressed him all the more because the expansion in the Soviet Union contrasted sharply with the mass unemployment of the Great Depression in the capitalist countries.

Of course Fischer had certain doubts: The first surfaced in June 1928 during the Shakhty trial, when Soviet engineers were falsely accused of sabotage and espionage. One of the accused, a certain Mushkin with a pale and pasty face, rattled off his tale like a prepared speech. Fischer realized that Mushkin was only playing a role rehearsed in the basement of the headquarters of the secret police. This was followed by Trotsky's banishment and later deportation. He saw that the revolver of the secret police had become the ultimate means of persuasion. Fischer witnessed an increase in the importance of the secret police in the Soviet state and noted with criticism the rise of "grovelling sycophants and the saccharin-sweet glorification of Josef Stalin." Fischer seemed close to finding his own Kronstadt, but he still hoped and believed that these were abscesses on an otherwise healthy body.

With the Nazi victory in Germany in 1933, Fischer's priorities began to shift dramatically. The mighty campaign for an anti-Fascist coalition, which was propagated by the People's Commissar for Foreign Affairs, Litvinov, stood in the forefront for Fischer. His assessment of Soviet domestic affairs was divided: On the one hand, living conditions had improved somewhat during 1934 and 1935, on the other hand, he saw clearly that the bureaucracy bred more and more sycophants, cynics, and cowards. The top as well as the bottom ranks were permeated by fear rather than creativity, and selfishness rather than concern for the common good—but especially fear. "These careful, calculating, obsequious, nervous dissemblers in the government administration, in the Party, in the unions and other organizations paid close attention to the steps they took, looking shyly over their shoulders and loudly proclaiming their loyalty. They monotonously recited the official propaganda and as a consolation ate, drank, danced and in general lived as luxuriously as the improved material conditions permitted."

Fischer was especially critical of the growing social differentiation, the fact that the unions were deprived of their rights while the factory directors were wheeling and dealing, hiring, and firing, and determining what salaries would be paid. After the murder of Sergei Kirov on December 1, 1934, 103 people were executed who had been imprisoned many months before

Kirov's death. Fischer was revolted: The Soviet state had grown into a horrible, gigantic monster. To this was added the growth of nationalism: The revolutionaries of the past were increasingly neglected, while more and more czars and czarist generals were turned into national heroes.

Fischer grasped at a shred of hope once more, in 1935, when it was announced that a new, "democratic" constitution was being prepared. But by 1936 the mass arrests and the Moscow show trials of the Great Purge began. Fischer felt that night was falling: He knew that he neither could nor wanted to live in the Soviet Union any longer.

At this critical moment, Franco organized his uprising, ushering in the Spanish Civil War. Spain became Fischer's battleground against Fascism. He left the Soviet Union and went to Spain, where he not only wrote on the war but actively participated in battle. The Spanish Civil War captivated all of his thoughts and actions and so again postponed his Kronstadt. Of course, Fischer learned from occasional trips to Moscow and from his friends in the Soviet Union about the Great Purge, and even in Spain he was not cut off from developments in the Soviet Union: Soviet citizens who served in Spain either as military advisors or as civilians were recalled to Moscow where they were arrested, banished, and sometimes even executed. However, Fischer found a way out of his dilemma: Despite all his criticism of the domestic situation in the Soviet Union, he could support Soviet foreign policy wholeheartedly. He remained silent because he didn't want to endanger the Soviet Union's anti-Fascist campaign. But his Kronstadt caught up with him:

> Then came the Soviet-Nazi pact of August 23, 1939, which put the Soviet government on the course which it has followed from that day until the present. This pact provoked my "Kron-

stadt." The pact was an agreement whose goal was not to gain time but the cession of territory. Secret but now published protocols delineated the spheres of influence in all those regions which Soviet-Nazi aggression could reach. With that began Russia's aggression which brought it the empire creaking in every joint which it has today and which made it the most evil problem for humanity. The Soviet-Nazi pact was the tombstone of the Bolshevik International and the cornerstone of Bolshevik imperialism. It was possible because Bolshevik Russia had become a cemetary for the Bolsheviks. I could not sympathize with a system which betrayed its origins and its creators.[11]

Willi Münzenberg: You, Stalin, Are the Traitor!

Among the many Communists who broke with the Soviet Union and the Comintern because of their disillusionment and indignation over the Hitler-Stalin pact, Willi Münzenberg was undoubtedly the most significant.

Münzenberg, who became a close friend of Lenin in 1917, founded the Communist Youth International and for two decades was probably the most competent director of propaganda in the international Communist movement. He was born in 1889 in Erfurt in Thuringia to poor parents and attended public school irregularly, but he secretly read everything he could get his hands on. As a youth he began working in a shoe factory in Erfurt and joined the Socialist Youth Federation. He went to Switzerland as a wandering apprentice and worked as a delivery boy for a pharmacy in Zurich. In 1915, he met the Russian emigrés who lived in Zurich during the First World War: Lenin and his wife Krupskaja, Trotsky, and Zinoviev. Münzenberg was active in the Socialist Youth Federation in Zurich and soon became its chairman. He went to Germany in 1918 and joined the CP Germany upon its foundation. However, he was especially active in the Communist youth movement. As a result, he founded the Communist Youth International together with Leo Flieg, the Austrian Richard Schüller, the Yugoslav Karlo Stajner, and the Swiss Paul Thalmann.[12] Münzenberg was elected Chairman of the Communist Youth International upon its foundation but soon protested at the interference from the Comintern and was removed by the head of the Comintern, G.Y. Zinoviev.

In the summer of 1921, Lenin—with whom Münzenberg either had corresponded or had been in personal contact the entire time—commissioned him to organize international aid for those suffering from famine in Russia. Münzenberg became the founder and organizer of the International Workers' Aid and was extremely successful: money and supplies worth millions came to Soviet Russia, which was ravaged by hunger. The International Workers' Aid began to support more and more Communists in many countries who were on strike or imprisoned, as well as their families.

Münzenberg did not participate in the factional struggles of the party or the Comintern and was relatively independent. His success was largely a result of his freedom from the crippling control of the party bureaucracy. As a result, he succeeded in founding newspapers, magazines, and film studios, and in organizing them with imagination. He was increasingly successful in convincing well-known intellectuals and famous personalities to contribute. As early as 1926, Münzenberg had two daily newspapers with a broad circulation, the *Welt am Abend* and *Berlin am Morgen*; another paper called the *Arbeiter-Illustrierte*; a magazine entitled *Roter Aufbau*, and others for photographers and radio amateurs, which cleverly included Communist views; a successful film studio; and a publishing house, the Neuer

Deutscher Verlag, with a series of popular books, the *Universum Bücherei*. Within a few years, Willi Münzenberg's International Workers' Aid had newspapers, magazines, fund-raising drives, soup kitchens, and children's homes throughout the entire world. Margarete Buber-Neumann, who knew him at the time, described him as follows:

> Willi Münzenberg was truly an astounding personality who had an almost magical influence on people from the most varied walks of life. . . . No other prominent German Communist was so full of ideas as Münzenberg. He remained true to the customs of the youth movement. On Sundays when there were no meetings to attend Willi Münzenberg went out into the countryside. . . . Münzenberg scarcely drank alcohol, loved hiking, camping in the forest and sports.[13]

With the founding of the Anti-Imperialist League in 1927, Münzenberg's name became known far beyond the borders of Germany. Other members of the League included Luis Carlos Prestes from Brazil; Jawaharlal Nehru, who later became the Prime Minister of India; the Mexican painter Diego Rivera; the widow of Sun-Yat-Sen; and General Sandino from Nicaragua, whom the Sandinistas considered their predecessor. The psychologist and writer Manes Sperber, who knew the forty-two-year-old Münzenberg in Berlin at the end of 1931, recalled: "His name had already penetrated far beyond the borders of Germany. Everywhere in the world, in the Communist movement and in the countless organizations sympathetic to the Communists, but especially among the intellectuals of many countries, the propagandist of the Comintern achieved astounding success under different names and with varied means."[14]

After Hitler seized power in 1933, Münzenberg transferred his activities to Paris and soon founded the Committee to Aid the Victims of German Fascism, with offices all over Europe and in the United States. In addition to the official committee, with international celebrities in its list of patrons, there was the secretariat proper, staffed by Münzenberg and other Communists. At first, their office was in the Rue Mendetour near les Halles, and later at No. 38 Boulevard Montparnasse. Soon thereafter, Münzenberg founded the Editions du Carrefour publishing house and published the famous *Brown Book on the Reichstag Fire and Hitler's Terror*, a harsh denunciation of the Nazi system, which was soon translated into many languages. The most important author of the *Brown Book* was Otto Katz, alias Andre Simon, who, at the end of 1952, was condemned to death during the Slansky trial in Czechoslovakia.

After publishing the *Brown Book*, Münzenberg founded the Committee for Investigating the Reasons Behind the Reichstag Fire Trial, which was composed of lawyers of international repute from different countries. This committee organized the famous "Counter Trial" shortly before the official Reichstag Fire Trial began in Germany, and thereby greatly embarrassed the Nazis. This was followed by the second "Brown Book," entitled *Dimitroff Against Göring—Revelations About the True Arsonists*, and by many other committees intended to aid in the struggle against Fascism as part of the recently announced Popular Front.

Münzenberg was called to Moscow in May 1936, where he was instructed to begin a new mass movement for peace. This new movement was named "Rassemblement Universel pour la Paix" (RUP) and was called the World Peace Movement (*Weltfriedensbewegung*) by the German emigrés in Paris. The organization's offices were in the Rue de Bourgogne in Paris. Münzenberg was instructed by Moscow to play down the Communist element in the movement and to convince prominent personalities to contribute their time and effort. In this, Münzenberg was surprisingly successful: The RUP Congress in Brussels on September 7 and 8, 1936, was attended by 5,500 delegates of various persuasions from many countries. The previously prepared resolution calling for "collective security and indivisible peace" was accepted by the delegates.

In the autumn of 1936, Münzenberg was still the director of the huge propaganda organization of the Comintern, but the end was approaching. That summer, Moscow had sent the Czech Comintern official Bohumil Smeral to Paris. Officially, Smeral was to work with Münzenberg, but his true task was to gradually eliminate Münzenberg and take charge of the organization himself.

In October 1936, Münzenberg was recalled to Moscow to work in the agitation and propaganda department of the Comintern. Münzenberg's trip to Moscow with his wife Babette Gross was their last. When they arrived in Moscow, they realized with horror that the wave of persecutions that followed Zinoviev's and Kamenev's death sentence had not subsided but only just begun. Babette Gross recalled: "People were bewildered. They couldn't understand what was happening and racked their brains to learn the deviations from the Party line of which they were guilty and of which they could now be accused during the Great Purge. . . . No one dared to visit us in our hotel, the newly built 'Moscow' on the Arbat." When Münzenberg tried to arrange a meeting with Karl Radek he was told by a former colleague, under pledge of secrecy, that Radek had just been arrested.

At the Comintern headquarters, Münzenberg was told that he should transfer his organization in Paris to Smeral, and was asked at the same time to appear before the International Control Commission of the Comintern to respond to charges that he allegedly "lacked revolutionary vigilance." Münzenberg was accused of employing a certain Liane Klein, whose father had allegedly spied for Franco and who had obtained information on the propaganda organization from his daughter. At first, Münzenberg was cheered by this accusation because Liane had only worked as a secretary in one of the offices from 1933 until 1935, and had never had any contact with confidential information. However, when Münzenberg was summoned a second and a third time for the same matter, he realized that it was all a pretense for eliminating him.

From then on, he had only one thought: to leave Moscow as quickly as possible. Münzenberg went to Togliatti and explained that it was absolutely necessary for him to bring the campaign for Spain, which he had started in Paris, to an end. Togliatti agreed, and Münzenberg was told by the Cadre Department of the Comintern that he and his wife Babette were permitted to leave. When Münzenberg took leave from Heinz Neumann, the latter began to weep; both knew that they would never see one another again.

At the appointed time, Willi Münzenberg and Babette Gross arrived at the railroad station where they waited in vain: No one came to give them their passports with their exit visas and train tickets. Downcast, they returned to their hotel. "That night we didn't sleep a wink, waiting for the NKVD (secret police) to knock at the door," recalled Babette Gross. The next morning, Münzenberg stormed into Togliatti's office and staged an angry scene, which had the desired effect. In Münzenberg's presence, Togliatti made a series of important telephone calls. Shortly thereafter, Willi Münzenberg and Babette Gross received their passports, visas, and tickets and departed from Moscow the same day.

Münzenberg returned to Paris via Denmark. "He had calmed down again after the hectic days in Moscow," wrote Babette Gross. "He would never again return to Moscow. Now it was important to continue to live and work without the support of the Comintern, yes in all probability against it."

Upon his arrival in Paris, Münzenberg handed over the reports, balance sheets, and accounts of all of the committees and publishing houses that he controlled to the Comintern's new deputy, Smeral. The enterprise that he had built up and which spanned the globe was taken over by the party bureaucracy and soon collapsed. At the same time, Münzenberg had an encounter which deeply shook him: Bukharin, once one of Lenin's closest comrades-in-arms and later chairman of the Communist International, had come to Paris to deliver a speech to the Society of Friends of Soviet Russia. It was excruciating. Bukharin was a broken man who read his manuscript and even whispered inaudibly during some portions of his talk. Then a telegram arrived from Moscow recalling Bukharin. In vain, his friends implored him to remain in Paris. As white as a ghost and with his voice breaking, Bukharin declared that he would return to Moscow, even though he knew exactly what awaited him.

In the spring of 1937, Münzenberg received a postcard from Moscow: Heinz Neumann had been arrested. A few days later, Leo Flieg, a well-known German CP official and an old friend of Münzenberg who resided in Paris, was also recalled to Moscow. Münzenberg and other friends advised him not to go. Leo Flieg defended himself with a calm voice: "I have nothing on my conscience. I won't back out!" He was arrested upon his arrival in Moscow.

Under these circumstances, the German Popular Front was founded at a meeting on April 10, 1937, in a hall on the Rue Cadet in Paris. Three hundred delegates of various political persuasions participated. The speakers included the author Heinrich Mann, the Social Democrat Rudolf Breitscheid, and Willi Münzenberg, who spoke on the tasks of the Popular Front. In apparent reference to the Communist leaders in Paris, he spoke against a narrow-minded policy of subterfuges, which only destroyed people's confidence. For this he was thanked conspicuously by Heinrich Mann, but behind the scenes Walter

Ulbricht intrigued against Münzenberg's participation in the Popular Front and thereby further weakened it.

As a result of the Great Purge in the Soviet Union and the purges in republican Spain, one group after another left the Popular Front—first the progressive liberals led by Leopold Schwarzschild and the magazine *Neue Tagebuch*, then the remainder of the Social Democrats, and finally the representatives of the Socialist Workers' party.

The emigré leaders of the CP Germany conducted a whispering campaign against Münzenberg from the autumn of 1937 until the autumn of 1938, while at the same time repeatedly urging him to go to Moscow. Dimitrov wrote to him that important new duties awaited him in Moscow. Münzenberg received a second letter from Dimitrov, who wrote that he completely understood the difficulties that Münzenberg had had in Paris but that everything could be solved as soon as Münzenberg was in Moscow, where they could speak their minds.

Soon thereafter, Münzenberg met an American Communist who asked, "What could happen to you?" But Münzenberg still refused: "They'll shoot me as they shot the others and ten years later explain that they made a big mistake." And so he chose to remain in Paris.

The Communist campaign against Münzenberg increased in the autumn of 1938. A circular distributed by the Communist faction in the Popular Front Committee reported that Münzenberg was being investigated for having talked with "rightist bourgeois elements" without having informed the party. In response to this campaign against him, Münzenberg distributed to his close friends a circular, which was not published, in which he announced, without acrimony and abuse, his resignation from the CP Germany: "Since the circumstances in Germany and the heightening of the international crisis require the commitment of each and every person, my political past, my sense of socialist responsibility and my temperament compel me to sever my links to an organization which makes political work for me impossible." In conclusion, he declared that his attitude toward the Soviet Union had not changed.[15]

Münzenberg founded the independent, nonpartisan German weekly *Die Zukunft*, whose first issue appeared in October of 1938. The goal of *Die Zukunft* was to continue the struggle against Nazism, to support cooperation between the various emigré groups, and to develop a program for the period after the collapse of the Nazi regime. Even the first issue included a list of contributors of all political persuasions: Thomas Mann, Heinrich Mann, Stefan Zweig, Josef Roth, Arnold Zweig, Lion Feuchtwanger, Alfred Döblin, Alfred Kerr, Rudolf Olden, Manes Sperber, and many foreigner writers, including Ignazio Silone and H. G. Wells. *Die Zukunft* was so successful that it far surpassed the magazine of the CP Germany, *Deutsche Volks-zeitung*.

At the beginning of 1939, a loose group called Friends of the Future was formed, which organized political discussions and which, through its cultural events, provided the German emigrés with a sort of intellectual focus. From this developed the Friends of Socialist Unity—groups of German emigrés with independent political ideas who, in close cooperation with Austrian emigrés, developed a program for a future, reformed German labor movement. The goal was the union of "all honest anti-Nazi workers" in a "united, revolutionary party of the working class" with the guaranteed right of "self determination" within the party and complete independence, not only from the Second (Socialist) International but from the Third (Communist) International, and the fundamental willingness to cooperate with "all the honest, democratic forces in Germany."

On March 10, 1939, Willi Münzenberg formally announced his reasons for resigning from the CP Germany in *Die Zukunft*:

"It is difficult for me to resign from an organization which I helped to found and create," he wrote. He recalled that as early as 1915, he was one of the first German socialists to join Lenin and his movement and that he had given everything to this movement for the past twenty-five years. During the last two years he had come into conflict with the emigré leaders of the CP Germany, in particular over the goals of the Popular Front and over democracy within the party. Münzenberg accused the CP Germany of a "contradictory policy": On the one hand it called for a democratic people's republic, while on the other it did not renounce a "one party dictatorship." The CP advocated the creation of a "united party of the working class," while at the same time continuing the old tactic of defamation. The struggle against Fascism was rendered more difficult "by an organizational form which has little in common with that of the original party, by the preponderance of the bureaucratic apparatus which dominates party life and by a party leadership which considers itself infallible and irreplaceable despite all of the defeats experienced since 1933."

Münzenberg did not limit himself to criticism, but also announced his own political goals: "The workers' party must avow the fundamental principles of the classic labor movement, the inviolable nature of democracy within the party and the right of all members to have a voice in decisions." The struggle against Fascism can only be won by people who are convinced of their own ideas and experience and who voluntarily accept suffering and sacrifice. The struggle cannot be won by regimented, commanded, and tormented souls. The essence of his view of the future of Germany after Hitler's downfall was as follows: "If the existence of the new Germany is to be justified, then it can neither be a schematic repetition of the Weimar democracy nor the domination by a single party according to the Stalinist pattern."

Nevertheless, even after he publicly announced his resignation from the CP Germany, Münzenberg avoided attacking Stalin and the Soviet Union: "I do not change my attitude towards the Soviet Union, the first country of socialism, the great guarantor of peace," Münzenberg wrote in his declaration of March 10, 1939. [16]

Then came the Hitler-Stalin pact. All of the reasons for remaining loyally silent about the Soviet Union disappeared. Babette Gross recalled that all of Münzenberg's dams broke. His protest was like a scream. Münzenberg exposed "the Russian stab in the back"; his article concluded with the following words:

> Peace and freedom must be defended—against Hitler and Stalin. We must fight for the victory against Hitler and Stalin and the new, independent united German labor party must be forged in battle against Hitler and against Stalin. . . . For years a mercenary press has incited and slandered, has spread hundreds of vile lies, and suspected thousands of courageous workers. Not a single number of the *Volkszeitung* has appeared which did not repeat a hundred times: "Down with the parasites, down with the traitors!" Today millions of people rise up in every country, stretch out their arms and call, pointing towards the East: "You Stalin, are the traitor!" [17]

Notes

Introduction

1. R. J. Sontag and J. S. Beddie, eds., *Nazi-Soviet Relations 1939–1941. Documents from the Archives of the German Foreign Office* (Washington, D.C., 1948).
2. J. V. Stalin, *Sochineniya*, vol. 6 (1924), p. 282.
3. *Sputnik*, no. 10, 1988, pp. 136–138.
4. Ibid., p. 10.

Chapter 1

1. Hans von Herwarth, *Zwischen Hitler und Stalin. Erlebte Zeitgeschichte 1931–1945* (Frankfurt/Main, 1982), p. 186.
2. A. Rossi, *Zwei Jahre deutsch-sowjetisches Bündnis* (Cologne, 1954), pp. 50–51. Stalin's toast is also quoted by Leopold Trepper, *The Great Game* (New York, 1977), p. 102.
3. Herwarth, pp. 187–189.
4. Rossi, p. 54.
5. Alexander Werth, *Russia at War 1941–1945* (New York, 1970), pp. 71–72. The text of the nonaggression pact has been published many times; see for example J. A. S. Grenville, *The Major International Treaties 1914–1973* (New York, 1974), pp. 195–196.

6. *Khrushchev Remembers* (Boston, 1970), pp. 127–129.

7. Ernst Fischer, *Erinnerungen und Reflexionen* (Reinbek bei Hamburg, 1969), pp. 406–409.

8. Jesus Hernandez, *La grande trahison* (Paris, 1953), pp. 206–207.

9. Enrique Castro Delgado, *Mi fe se perdio en Moscu* (Mexico City, 1951), pp. 36–37.

10. Castro Delgado, p. 37.

11. Fischer, pp. 409–411.

12. Ruth von Mayenburg, *Blaues Blut und Rote Fahnen* (Vienna-Munich-Zurich, 1969), p. 268.

13. Friedrich Uttitz, *Zeugen der Revolution. Mitkämpfer Lenins und Stalins berichten* (n.d.), p. 134.

14. Herbert Wehner, *Zeugnis* (Cologne, n.d.), p. 233.

15. Sidney Wilfred Scott, *Rebel in a Wrong Cause* (Auckland, 1960), pp. 104–105.

16. Castro Delgado, pp. 43–46.

17. Herwarth, p. 173.

18. Herwarth, pp. 187–188.

19. Juho Kusti Paasikivi, *Meine Moskauer Mission 1939–1941* (Hamburg, 1966), pp. 50–51, 56.

20. Paasikivi, p. 58.

21. Grigore Gafencu, *Prelude to the Russian Campaign* (London, 1945), pp. 40, 42–44.

22. Werth, pp. 72–73.

23. Castro Delgado, pp. 45–46.

24. Werth, p. 74.

25. Werth, p. 75; N. G. Kuznetsov, *Am Vorabend* (East Berlin, 1969), pp. 250–253.

26. Grenville, p. 196.

27. Rossi, p. 54.

28. Alexander Nekrich, *Entsage der Angst. Erinnerungen eines Historikers* (Frankfurt/Main-Berlin-Vienna, 1983), p. 143.

CHAPTER 2

1. Werth, p. 72.

2. *Manchester Guardian*, August 25, 1939, p. 6; *Times* (London), August 28, 1939, p. 9.

3. Oksana Kasenkina, *Leap to Freedom* (New York, 1949), p. 86.

4. Anatoli Granovsky, *I was an NKVD Agent* (New York, 1962), p. 120.

5. M. I. Gallai, "The Strange Twenty-two Months," in *Stalin and his Generals. Soviet Military Memoirs of World War II*, ed. Seweryn Bialer (New York, 1969), p. 128.

6. Victor Kravchenko, *I Chose Freedom* (New York, 1946), pp. 332–335.

7. Leopold Grünwald, *Wandlung: Ein Altkommunist gibt zu Protokoll* (Vienna, n.d.), p. 71.

8. Wolfgang Leonhard, *Child of the Revolution* (London, 1957), pp. 62–68.

9. Kravchenko, p. 334.

10. Leonhard, pp. 73–74.

11. Castro Delgado, pp. 38–39.

12. Leonhard, p. 75.

13. Herbert Wehner, *Zeugnis* (Cologne, 1982), pp. 233–234.

14. Werth, p. 63.

15. Leonhard, p. 73.

16. Joseph Berger, *Nothing But the Truth* (New York, 1971), p. 177.

17. Roy Medvedev, *Let History Judge. The Origins and Consequences of Stalinism* (New York, 1971), p. 443.

18. Kravchenko, p. 335.

19. Joseph Stalin, *The Great Patriotic War of the Soviet Union* (New York, 1945), p. 11.

20. Medvedev, p. 444.

21. Alexander Weissberg, *The Accused* (New York, 1951), pp. 469, 482–483, 495, 502, 504–506. The conversations with the Bashkir and with the diplomat from Chung King are mentioned but not quoted in the English edition.

22. Eugenia Ginzburg, *Journey Into the Whirlwind* (New York, 1967), pp. 367–368.

23. Margarete Buber, *Under Two Dictators* (New York, n.d.), pp. 138, 159, 162, 165–166.

CHAPTER 3

1. *The Communist International. A Short Historical Outline* (East Berlin, 1970), p. 544.

2. Willi Dickhut, *So war das damals. Tatsachenbericht eines Solinger Arbeiters 1926–1948* (Stuttgart, 1979), pp. 262–264.

3. Eugen Eberle and Peter Grohmann, *Die schlaflosen Nächte des Eugen E. Erinnerungen eines neuen schwäbischen Jakobiners* (Stuttgart, 1982), p. 99.

4. Paul Elflein, *Immer noch Kommunist?*, ed. Rolf Becker and Claus Bremer (Hamburg, 1978), pp. 101–102.

5. Erich Honecker, *From My Life* (New York, 1981), p. 102.

6. Heinz Brandt, *Ein Traum, der nicht entführbar ist. Mein Weg zwischen Ost und West* (Munich, 1967), pp. 133–140.

7. Eugen Ochs, *Ein Arbeiter im Widerstand* (Stuttgart, 1984), p. 40.

8. Wolfgang Abendroth, *Ein Leben in der Arbeiterbewegung* (Frankfurt/Main, 1976), pp. 180–181.

9. Franz Dahlem, *Am Vorabend des Zweiten Weltkrieges*, vol. 2 (East Berlin, n.d.), pp. 377–379, 381.

10. Alexander Abusch, *Der Deckname. Memoirs* (East Berlin, 1984), p. 481.

11. Abusch, p. 482.

12. The statement of the Central Committee of the CP Germany of August 25, 1939, was published in the *Rundschau*, no. 46 (Basel, 1939), pp. 1323–1324. See also Horst Duhnke, *Die KPD von 1933–1945* (Cologne, 1972), pp. 334–335; Julius Braunthal, *Geschichte der Internationale*, vol. 1 (Hannover, 1963), pp. 517–518; and the memoir of Alexander Abusch, pp. 48–49.

13. Abusch, pp. 483–484.

14. Henry Jacoby, *Davongekommen. 10 Jahre Exil 1936–1946* (Frankfurt/Main, 1982), p. 73.

15. Jacoby, p. 104.

16. Jacoby, pp. 101–105.

17. Jürgen Kuczynski, *Memoiren. Die Erziehung des J. K. zum Kommunisten und Wissenschaftler* (East Berlin, 1975), p. 287.

18. Theodor Balk, *Das verlorene Manuskript* (Mexico City, 1943; reprint ed., Hildesheim, 1979), pp. 190, 194–197, 199, 203–205, 207–209.

19. Hasso Grabner and Heinz Mildner, *Der Weg nach Hause. Erinnerungen von Generalmajor Ewald Munschke* (East Berlin, 1963), p. 147.

20. Heinz Kühn, *Widerstand und Emigration. Die Jahre 1928–1945* (Hamburg, 1980), pp. 227–229.

21. Karl Kunde, *Die Odyssee eines Arbeiters* (Stuttgart, 1985), pp. 47–49, 134–135.

22. *Süddeutsche Volksstimme* (Zurich, 1939), quoted in Hans Teubner, *Exilland Schweiz* (East Berlin, 1975; reprint ed., Frankfurt/Main, 1975), p. 58.

23. Teubner, pp. 56–60.

24. Karl Mewis, *Im Auftrag der Partei* (East Berlin, 1972), pp. 214, 220–224.

25. *Rundschau über Politik, Wirtschaft und Arbeiterbewegung. Informationsorgan der Kommunistischen Internationale*, 8, Jahrgang no. 13 (Basel, March 14, 1939), p. 862.

26. Charles Tillon, *On Chantait Rouge* (Paris, 1977), p. 278.

27. Giulio Ceretti, *A l'Ombre des Deux T* (Paris, 1973), p. 196.

28. Adam Raysky, *Nos Illusions Perdues* (Paris, 1985), p. 64.

29. Clara and Paul Thalmann, *Revolution für die Freiheit. Stationen eines politischen Kampfes: Moskau, Madrid, Paris* (Hamburg, 1976), p. 258, reprint of the first edition published under the title *Wo die Freiheit Stirbt* (Olten, 1974).

30. Tillon, p. 280.

31. A. Rossi, *Les Communistes Francais Pendant la Drole de Guerre* (Paris, 1951), p. 36.

32. Marcel Thourel, *Itineraire d'un Cadre Communiste* (Toulouse, 1980), pp. 113–115.

33. George Cogniot, *Zwiesprache mit meinem Leben. Weg und Ziel eines französischen Patrioten und Kommunisten* (East Berlin, 1983), p. 345.

34. Dahlem, pp. 371, 386.

35. Tillon, pp. 282, 284.

36. Girgio Amendola, *Der Antifaschismus in Italien. Ein Interview* (Stuttgart, 1977), pp. 158, 160.

37. Amendola, p. 164 and notes on p. 242.

38. Teresa Noce, *Estella. Autobiographie einer italienischen Revolutionärin* (Frankfurt/Main, 1981), pp. 211–213, 237–238, Italian original is entitled *Rivoluzionaria Professionale* (Milan, 1974).

39. Ilya Ehrenburg, *Memoirs: 1921–1941* (New York, 1966), pp. 471–472.

40. *Rundschau über Politik, Wirtschaft und Arbeiterbewegung. Informationsorgan der Kommunistischen Internationale*, 8, Jahrgang no. 13 (Basel, March 14, 1939), p. 862.

41. Edith Bone, *7 Years Solitary* (New York, 1957), pp. 38–40.

42. Douglas Hyde, *I Believed* (New York, 1950), pp. 71–72.

43. Franz Loeser, *Sag nie, Du gehst den letzten Weg* (Cologne, 1986), pp. 32–34, 39–40.

44. Antonio Pesenti, *La Cattedra e il Bugliolo* (Milan, 1972), pp. 185–187.

45. Zoltan Vas, *Hazateres 1944 (The Return Home 1944)* (Budapest, 1970), pp. 22–24.

46. Vladimir Dedijer, *Tito Speaks* (London, 1953), p. 124.

47. Milovan Djilas, *Memoir of a Young Revolutionary* (New York, 1973), pp. 329–330.

48. Svetozar Vukmanovic-Tempo, *Mein Weg mit Tito. Ein Revolutionär erinnert sich* (Munich-Zurich, 1972), p. 66.

49. Vilko Vinterhalter, *Tito—der Wege des Josip Broz* (Vienna-Frankfurt-Zurich, 1969), pp. 158–162.

50. Jiri Pelikan, *Ein Frühling, der nie zu Ende geht. Erinnerungen eines Prager Kommunisten* (Frankfurt/Main, 1976), pp. 30–31.

51. Gusta Fucikowa, *Mein Leben mit Julius Fucik* (East Berlin, 1976), p. 384.

52. Leopold Trepper, *The Great Game* (New York, 1977), pp. 102–104.

53. Ruth Seydewitz, *Alle Menschen haben Träume. Meine Zeit, mein Leben* (East Berlin, 1978), pp. 322–323. Max Seydewitz only hints at these discussions in Loka Brunn in his memoirs, entitled *Es hat sich gelohnt zu leben. Erkenntnisse und Bekenntnisse* (East Berlin, 1976), pp. 401–402.

54. Walther Bringolf, *Mein Leben. Weg und Umweg eines Schweizer Sozialdemokraten* (Bern-Munich-Vienna, 1965), pp. 208–210.

55. Jules Humbert-Droz, *Dix ans de lutte antifasciste. 1931–1941*, vol. 3 (La Chatelle, 1972), pp. 386–387.

56. Friedrich Uttiz, *Zeugen der Revolution. Mitkämpfer Lenins und Stalins berichten* (1984), p. 112.

57. Ruth Werner, *Sonjas Rapport* (East Berlin, 1977), pp. 225–229, 231–235, 241–242.

58. Alexander Foote, *Handbook for Spies* (London, 1953), pp. 34–35.

59. George Charney, *A Long Journey* (Chicago, 1968), pp. 123–127.

60. Peggy Dennis, *The Autobiography of an American Communist: A Personal View of Political Life, 1925–1975* (Westport, 1977), pp. 132–137.

61. Klaus Mehnert, *Ein Deutscher in der Welt. Erinnerungen 1906–1981* (Stuttgart, 1981), p. 231.

62. John Gates, *The Story of an American Communist* (New York, 1958), pp. 74–76.

63. Leon Trotsky, *Writings of Leon Trotsky* (New York, 1978), pp. 79–80.

64. Alice Rühle-Gerstel, *Kein Gedicht für Trotzki. Tagebuchaufzeichnungen aus Mexiko* (Frankfurt/Main, 1979), pp. 12–17.

65. Isaac Deutscher, *Trotsky*, vol. 3, *The Prophet Outcast, 1929–1940* (London and New York, 1963), p. 361.

66. "After the Collapse of Czechoslovakia, Stalin will Seek Accord with Hitler," first published in *Socialist Appeal*, October 8, 1938; reprinted in *Writings of Leon Trotsky (1938–1939)* (New York, 1974), pp. 29–30.

67. Victor Serge, *The Life and Death of Leon Trotsky* (New York, 1975), p. 251.

68. Serge, p. 252.

69. "Stalin—Hitler's Quartermaster," written on September 2, 1939, published in *Socialist Appeal*, September 11, 1939; reprinted in *Writings of Leon Trotsky (1939–1940)* (New York, 1973), p. 80.

70. "Moscow is Mobilizing," written on September 11, 1939, pub-

lished in *Socialist Appeal*, September 15, 1939; reprinted in *Writings of Leon Trotsky (1939–1940)*, p. 87.

71. Deutscher, p. 458.

72. "Stalin—Temporary Holder of the Ukraine," written on September 18, 1939, published in *Socialist Appeal*, October 24, 1939; reprinted in *Writings of Leon Trotsky (1939–1940)*, p. 90.

73. Trotsky, pp. 91–92.

74. V. I. Lenin, *Left-Wing Communism, An Infantile Disorder* (New York, 1940), pp. 21–23.

75. Wolfgang Leonhard, *Schein und Wirklichkeit in der Sowjetunion* (West Berlin, 1952), pp. 112–114.

Chapter 4

1. Abusch, p. 484.

2. Hans Werner Richter, *Brief an einen jungen Sozialisten* (Hamburg, 1974), p. 79.

3. Granville Hicks, *Where We Came Out* (New York, 1954), pp. 7–8, 77, 80–81.

4. Arthur Koestler, *The God That Failed* (New York, 1949), pp. 22–23.

5. Ibid., pp. 60–61.

6. Ibid., pp. 63–64.

7. Arthur Koestler, *The Invisible Writing* (New York, 1954), pp. 369–370.

8. Koestler, *The God That Failed*, pp. 73–74.

9. Richter, pp. 37–38, 42–43, 50–51, 78–79. For his reaction to the Hitler-Stalin pact, see pp. 80–84.

10. Wolfgang Leonhard, *Völker Hört die Signale. Die Gründerjahre des Weltkommunismus* (1984), pp. 317–318.

11. Louis Fischer, "The God That Failed," in *Men and Politics: Europe Between the Two World Wars*, 2nd ed. (New York, 1966), pp. 603, 607–611.

12. Clara and Paul Thalmann, *Revolution für die Freiheit* (1976); Karlo Stajner, *7000 Tage in Sibirien* (1975). See especially Stajner's last book, *Povratak iz Gulaga*.

13. Margarete Buber-Neumann, *Von Potsdam nach Moskau* (Stuttgart, 1958), pp. 196–200.

14. Manes Sperber, *Die vergebliche Warnung* (Vienna, 1975; reprint ed., Munich, 1979), p. 189.

15. Babette Gross, *Willi Münzenberg. Eine politische Biographie* (Stuttgart, 1969), p. 316.

16. Gross, p. 318.

17. Gross, pp. 327–328.

ABOUT THE AUTHOR

Since his escape from East Berlin in 1949, Wolfgang Leonhard has been considered one of the world's foremost authorities on communism and the Soviet Union, lecturing at universities and foreign policy institutes worldwide. He has also worked in several capacities for NATO and the United States government and is the author of numerous books, including *The Kremlin and the West, Euro-communism: A Challenge to East and West*, and *Three Faces of Marxism*. Mr. Leonhard, who taught Soviet history at Yale University from 1966 through 1987, is now retired and resides in Eifel, West Germany. He is a member of the Council on Foreign Relations, and is a frequent contributor to *Foreign Affairs*.